Jack's

HANDY LIST OF IDIOMS

• Volume 1 •
– L

Other Titles by
JACK FORBES

Jack's Handy List of Idioms: Volume M – Z

*Jack's Handy List of Words—607 Words That
You Can't (or Shouldn't) Live Without*

*Natural Law and Inalienable Human Rights:
A Pathway to Freedom and Liberty*

Jack's

HANDY LIST OF IDIOMS

• Volume 1 •
– L

JACK FORBES

JAFO PUBLISHING

Lancaster, CA

For information about this title or to order other books and/or electronic media, contact the publisher:

JAFO PUBLISHING
2010 West Avenue K, PMB 520
Lancaster, CA 93536
www.JafoPublishing.com

Cover original artwork by Jack Forbes © 2022

Cover and interior design by The Book Cover Whisperer:
OpenBookDesign.biz

979-8-9868774-2-6 Paperback
979-8-9868774-4-0 eBook

Printed in the United States of America

FIRST EDITION

DEDICATION

This **Volume 1 (# – L)** book is somewhat of a *sequel* to my prior book, **Jack's Handy List of Words**, but it goes well beyond individual words and dives into the rich *culture and history* of American English. So, I dedicate each volume of **Jack's Handy List of Idioms** to both of my parents, Jack and Tottie.

Together, they not only brought me into this world, but also provided for me innumerable life opportunities. Their guidance and efforts allowed me to experience a wide diversity of education, sports, leisure activity, work, personal relationships and creative interests which, in turn, coalesced to supply the fodder for my writing acumen, personal exploits and good-hearted mischief. Thank you from the bottom of my heart, mom and dad.

CONTENTS

• PREFACE •

IDIOMS ARE METAPHORICAL FIGURES of speech with *non-literal* meanings. They add considerable variety and culture to any language. Here, I've endeavored to showcase the most interesting of English language idioms, with the goal of making them understandable and useful for you. These phrases, and the sometimes slang which they incorporate, give a welcome *breath of fresh air* to communication, thoughtfully enriching it with colorful content.

So, *that's that.* You might even say that these are *the best of the best*! Sit back and renew or learn *from whole cloth* this wonderful collection of idioms. In this book, words, or a combination of words, separated by a / are used in the alternative. For example, "Back on your/my feet" could be stated as "Back on your feet" or "Back on my feet".

To help you along, and to add a pinch of pure, unadulterated fun, I will use **each of the idioms** in a humorous or an otherwise engaging sentence. **Enjoy!**

What follows is Volume 1 of *the meat & potatoes*
(since it *is* true that, there's *no*
time like the present!)

# #

24/7

Meaning: All day, every day; 24-hours a day, seven-days a week.

Example: *The local mini-mart was open 24/7, much to the delight of patrons with the late-night munchies.*

The $64,000 question

Meaning: The heart of the issue; the pivotal issue to grasp and resolve.

Example: *Brills Gustafson had timely filed for unemployment benefits, but the $64,000 question was whether his employer would agree that no further work on acceptable terms had been offered, or, alternatively, that Brills had simply declined to accept further employment.*

7th inning stretch

Meaning: A baseball idiom for the period of time between the top of the 7th inning and the bottom of the 7th inning in a baseball game, where the spectators may stand and sing the song, *Take Me Out to the Ball Game.*

Example: *During the 7th inning stretch, my 4-year-old son and I sang, Take Me Out to the Ball Game, together, and I'll never forget that moment in our lives.*

800-pound gorilla

Meaning: An unyielding and massive force in any circumstance.

Example: *As it turned out, the 800-pound gorilla in this transaction was a 12-year-old girl who was the creator of the new board-game known as, "Escape!"*

86'd/to 86 (someone)

Meaning: To "throw" someone out of an establishment such as a tavern.

Example: *In Aspen, Colorado, I walked into a bar with a fake I.D., but when the bartender took one look at my 16-year-old face, I was 86'd in a hurry.*

Abandon ship

Meaning: Give up on the project or activity, immediately, due to some perceived danger.

Example: *When Annabelle hustled after them boys for playin' tag after dark, one of 'em yelled, "Abandon ship!" and they all took off runnin'.*

A bone to pick with (someone)

Meaning: A grievance one has with someone.

Example: *Considering that you single-handedly consumed all of the taters, yes, I suppose I rightly do got a bone to pick with you.*

Bone up

Meaning: To learn something quickly or refresh one's recollection on something.

Example: *Before traveling to the French Alps for a ski vacation, I was determined to bone up on my conversational French—mais certainement!*

Above board

Meaning: Honest and transparent.

Example: *As the Wall Street executive was walked out in handcuffs, he pleaded to his firm's minions, "You've got to believe that every trade I made was completely above board!"*

Above the law

Meaning: Claiming to be not bound by the proscriptions of law in the same manner as common people.

Example: *Apparently, the minivan driver felt she was above the law when she parked in a Handicap parking space with neither the slightest remorse nor consciousness of guilt.*

Above suspicion

Meaning: So known and well-respected as to be considered as beyond reproach.

Example: *The veteran hockey coach was loved by parents and competitors alike and was truly and in fact, above suspicion.*

Ace in the hole

Meaning: A decisive and as yet not revealed key advantage.

Example: *When the Governor's indiscretion was witnessed first-hand by his young assistant, Maribel, his ace in the hole was her insatiable political ambitions.*

Achilles' heel

Meaning: An inherent and decisive weakness; often a hidden vulnerability.

Example: *Reginald wanted to run for public office, but his*

Achilles heel was an extensive juvenile record of burglaries that somehow would be leaked to the press.

Add insult to injury

Meaning: Worsen the damage by an incidental offending act.

Example: *Following the accidental discharge of the veteran officer's firearm, the Media-release by his department chief only added insult to injury by referencing his advanced age.*

Afraid of (one's) own shadow

Meaning: Timid, weak, spineless.

Example: *When it got down to brass tacks, the President was afraid of his own shadow and surrounded himself with people to shield him from direct criticism.*

Ahead of the game

Meaning: Succeeding in a venture or activity at an above-average level.

Example: *The nubile young con artist was markedly ahead of the game as she lured her unsuspecting mark into investing heavily on the scam-trading platform.*

(It) ain't over 'til the fat lady sings

Meaning: The situation is not resolved until the very end.

Example: *Knowing his conviction would almost certainly be reversed on appeal, the mobster gloated as he addressed the sentencing Judge, "All I gots ta say, Your Highness, is that it ain't over 'til the fat lady sings!"*

(It) ain't over 'til it's over

Meaning: The situation is not resolved until the very end.

Example: *The kid from Jersey looked his mama straight in the eye and told her, "It ain't over 'til it's over," and then turned to his papa to plead his case for an allowance raise.*

Air-mailed (one's) shot

Meaning: A ball that sails well beyond its intended target area.

Example: *The PGA rookie yelled, "Fore, long" when he air-mailed his second shot past the 18th green.*

Alive and kicking

Meaning: Still living and active.

Example: *When the attractive young nurse touched his arm and inquired, "How are you feeling today, Mister Pennypacker?", the old coot gave a little whoop and replied, "Miss Periwinkle, I'm still alive and kicking!"*

All at sea

Meaning: Lost and confused.

Example: *Thirty minutes into the first day of Calculus, everyone in the class, save Percival Youngblood, was all at sea.*

All chiefs and no Indians

Meaning: Too many people trying to lead the activity and not enough people to implement it and keep it working.

Example: *It was a classic case of all chiefs and no Indians as the*

Plainville PTA had no consensus and failed to properly organize the annual Halloween festival.

All hands, on deck

Meaning: Everyone must pitch in and help.

Example: *To complete the elaborate holiday decorations by Christmas Eve, it was all hands, on deck in the Landgraf household.*

All hat and no cattle

Meaning: A poser with all pretense and little or no substance.

Example: *The Hollywood cowboy was all hat and no cattle as he attempted to mount his horse from the right side.*

All hell broke loose

Meaning: Whatever it is, just became a catastrophe.

Example: *When the arch rival biker gangs simultaneously arrived at the Guilty as Charged Roadhouse, all hell broke loose.*

All was/was not peaches and cream

Meaning: Everything's okay; or, everything is not okay.

Example: *When Manuel stumbled dead drunk through the front door at 3:23 a.m., Rosario made it perfectly clear that all was not peaches and cream.*

All that glitters is not gold

Meaning: Appearances of tranquility and wealth can be very deceiving.

Example: *The penniless waif from Nebraska finally arrived at Hollywood & Vine, only to learn that all that glitters is not gold.*

All the same

Meaning: Regardless of the context and circumstances.

Example: *While I appreciate the honor of being awarded this trophy for lifetime achievement in coaching, if it's all the same, I'll pass the trophy along to the youth baseball museum to honor all of the parents who gave their children the right and opportunity to compete.*

All's well that ends well

Meaning: If the end result is not too bad, then we can overlook minor difficulties along the way.

Example: *Despite three errors in the field and an "o-fer" batting fiasco, young Mario Esperanza threw his glove in the sky, exclaiming, "All's well that ends well" as his team won the game, 5 to 4.*

All the time in the world

Meaning: As much time as someone would need for the task.

Example: *Once the fighter had been unintentionally punched below the belt, the Referee gave him all the time in the world to recover and resume the match.*

Along those lines

Meaning: Within the same or similar general circumstances as described.

Example: *It was along those lines that I accepted the opportunity to become a government informant to expose the lies and treachery of both the gain-of-function lab and the complicity of the worldwide health organization which provided continued funding and logistical support.*

Ambulance chaser

Meaning: An attorney who generally limits their law practice to run-of-the-mill personal injury claims and cases.

Example: *Jordi never imagined becoming an ambulance chaser for a living, but after law school and passing the Bar, it seemed to pay the bills quite nicely.*

An E-ticket ride

Meaning: The best, most exciting of experiences.

Example: *Having finally purchased the car of his dreams, Oliver treated Penelope to an E-ticket ride through the winding mountain-roads of the Angeles Crest Forest.*

Another day, another dollar

Meaning: Every day, we can make a little profit if we keep working.

Example: *She handed him his cup of hot chocolate as he collapsed on an overstuffed chair and softly told her, "Another day, another dollar."*

Another shot

Meaning: An additional attempt.

Example: *After laying off surfing for some five years, I felt like* *a kook in the water, but wanted to give it another shot to see if I enjoy the sport again.*

Ante up

Meaning: Throw in your share of the work or, especially, the financial burden.

Example: *Billy Perkins glanced sideways at Manfred Thomas, and told him, "Ante up, Manfred, or we ain't gonna have enough gas to get to the rodeo an' back."*

Any port in the storm

Meaning: When you're desperate, any safe space or place or friendly face is a blessing, regardless of how uncomfortable or generally unattractive.

Example: *When the astronaut jury-rigged a plug, stopping the air-leak from Apollo 12, he reported back, "Houston, it's only a temporary fix, but any port in the storm."*

Appearances can be deceiving

Meaning: Things are not always as they seem.

Example: *The real reason most accomplished martial artists are reluctant to get into street fights is that they've all experienced first-hand that appearances can be deceiving and you never really know what you're getting yourself into.*

The apple doesn't fall far from the tree

Meaning: Direct descendants are quite commonly greatly influenced in their actions by their parents.

Example: *Sentencing the young bank robber, the sentient*

Judge leaned forward, tipped down his eyeglasses and remarked, "Mister Glass, considering that only a short two years ago I sentenced your father, Edward Glass, to fifteen years in State Prison for armed bank robbery, it appears that the apple doesn't fall far from the tree."

Armed to the teeth
Meaning: Heavily armed with effective weapons.
Example: *The brave young girls were armed to the teeth with boxes and bath towels as they converged on the bathroom to apprehend the pesky mouse.*

Around the horn
Meaning: A baseball term describing a situation after getting a first or second "out" with no one on base, where the baseball is thrown between the infielders before being tossed by the Third Baseman to the Pitcher.
Example: *Only one out away from a no-hitter, the Tar Heels Catcher started the ball around the horn for the charged-up infield.*

As blind as a bat
Meaning: Almost completely blind or absolutely blind.
Example: *The old bag was blind as a bat, but she always took the time of checking up on me when I was sick as a dog and home in self-isolation.*

As graceful as a hog on ice
Meaning: Exceptionally awkward.

Example: *The CEO was as graceful as a hog on ice as he boarded the Gulfstream IV jet, stumbling no fewer than three times.*

Asleep at the wheel
Meaning: Not paying proper attention to what one is doing.

Example: *The esteemed Foreman of this residential construction project was obviously asleep at the wheel, unless it makes sense for wallboard to go up before the electrical contractor finishes his work.*

As poor as a church mouse
Meaning: Living hand-to-mouth; very poor.

Example: *The street beggar appeared to be as poor as a church mouse, but when the homeless girl gave him $5 for food, he gave her $500 for her selfless generosity.*

As right as rain
Meaning: Close to the best, if not the best, a thing can be.

Example: *Actor Melody Mavins was right as rain as she stepped onto the set, in character, as Princess Diane.*

As the crow flies
Meaning: If in a straight line from point "A" to point "B."

Example: *As the crow flies, my second condo was only ten miles, at most, from the first, but in typical Bangkok traffic, it was a good hour and ten minutes away.*

At death's door

> **Meaning:** In such bad shape, health or condition as to be perilously close to death.
>
> **Example:** *The warm-hearted spinster was at death's door as several of her closest friends gathered nearby to express their sadness and condolences.*

(Doing something) at the drop of a hat

> **Meaning:** Engaging in activity in a spontaneous and last-minute manner.
>
> **Example:** *When Miniature Golf was suggested as the evening activity, at the drop of a hat the two young couples jumped in the '64 Chevy convertible to compete for the Best Putter title.*

At the end of the day

> **Meaning:** A *massively* overused idiom for, when all else is taken into account.
>
> **Example:** *At the end of the day, a few exceptional golf shots can erase the memory of an otherwise pathetic round.*

At the end of (one's) rope

> **Meaning:** Seemingly out of options and solutions.
>
> **Example:** *Suddenly, Snidely Tigenhalter found himself at the end of his rope as the Spinster Wellenhooper overwhelmed him with a brilliant five-jump checkers move.*

At the top of (one's) lungs

> **Meaning:** To verbalize something as loudly as physically possible.

Example: *At the top of his lungs, the First Mate hollered to the pirate crew, "Batten down the hatches me boys, there be a squall out thar!"*

Backhand compliment

Meaning: An insult, thinly disguised as a compliment.

Example: *Penny handed him a backhand compliment by commenting that his balding head made his face look fuller.*

Back in the day

Meaning: An expression used (often, over-used) by an older person reminiscing back to things as they were say, a decade or more ago.

Example: *Back in the day, I didn't have this pot belly and I actually had a full head of hair.*

Back on track

Meaning: A resumption of normality.

Example: *This is how it is and how we get this show back on track, so let's make it happen.*

Back on your/my feet

Meaning: Recovered from some hard times, sickness or disability.

Example: *After a few short weeks of sometimes arduous physical therapy, Mortimer was back on his feet again.*

Back-to-back

Meaning: Repeating instances of some occurrence, one after the other.

Example: *The Long Beach All-Stars had back-to-back victories in the international championship finals, thanks to their tireless training and excellent management and coaching staff.*

Back to square one

Meaning: Having failed to accomplish the task, the process is started all over again.

Example: *Once the would-be bank robbers realized their drills could not penetrate the concrete flooring, it was back to square one.*

Back to the drawing board

Meaning: After a snafu of one sort or another, returning to the planning mode.

Example: *The detention students went back to the drawing board once their fire-drill escape plan failed miserably.*

A bad apple

Meaning: A defective, corrupt or dishonest person within an otherwise cordial, cooperative and fair-minded group of people.

Example: *The bad apples undermined the legitimacy of the* *protest when they turned it into a destructive and highly offensive melee.*

A bad beat

Meaning: A poker term for, a very good poker hand being defeated at showdown because of an extremely unlikely card having been dealt at or near the final card of the common cards.

Example: *The six on the River was a bad beat for Reginald "Aces-Up" Watkins, who now was down to seven big blinds, heads up, on tilt, with the tournament win virtually out of reach.*

Bad blood

Meaning: Existing animosity between two persons or groups, generated from earlier dealings.

Example: *The Tehachapi Ticks and Bakersfield Bees had bad blood ever since a controversy about whether B17 had actually been called in the finals of a Bingo championship, but the teams learned to let bygones be bygones in their latest, uneventful Bingo tournament.*

A bad egg

Meaning: An unpleasant person.

Example: *Except for the bad egg loitering off to one side, the party guests were both boisterous and elated to be at Brandy's college-acceptance gathering.*

(To) bad mouth (someone)

Meaning: To criticize someone, typically behind their back.

Example: *It was one thing to bad mouth the head of the carpet layers' union, but to send him shredded scraps of carpet with a note of "You're next!" was way out of hand.*

A bad workman blames his tools

Meaning: If a person wrongly attributes failure to the tools of his or her trade, it probably means that the person him/herself is incompetent.

Example: *As the disgruntled Tour player missed the cut and repeatedly slammed his 7-iron into his bag, the television announcer appropriately observed, "A bad workman blames his tools."*

Bag of bones

Meaning: Exceptionally skinny, malnourished and frail.

Example: *When the Oscar-nominated actor completed his final scene in Camps of Death, the production crew broke into spontaneous applause for the veritable bag of bones.*

Bait and switch

Meaning: A tactic of luring someone in with a high-quality item and then precipitously substituting another item of a considerably lower quality.

Example: *Belinda Postlethwaite had a penchant for deception and was a Zen Master of the bait and switch on various dating sites.*

Baked into the cake

Meaning: An integral part of the overall plan.

Example: *Nerves are already baked into the cake when competing at this level, but once a swimmer hits the water, it's game on!*

Balance the books

Meaning: To bring opposing interests into equilibrium.

Example: *Mob boss Patrick Murphy ordered the hit on Tony "the Nose" Palmetto to balance the books after their own Denny O'Sullivan was brutally gunned down.*

Bald-faced liar/lie

Meaning: A person who is an unrepentant purveyor of falsehoods, or a complete lie.

Example: *With a straight face, this bald-faced liar told the jury that I had been the aggressor, but he pronto changed his tune when the exculpatory video was produced during cross-examination.*

The ball is in (someone's) court

Meaning: The next move is yours.

Example: *Once I had sent condolences to my arch enemy for his cancer diagnosis, the ball was in his court to let bygones be bygones.*

The ball never lies

Meaning: After a controversial call, the next victory is usually an indicator of what the prior call should have been.

Example: *Henry Upton was successful in claiming beer pong interference but the ball never lies and his replay was a goose-egg.*

Ballpark figure/estimate

Meaning: A good faith, rough estimate taking many pertinent factors into account.

Example: *Tom's estimate of ten grand to convert my car to its spec-racing version could not fairly be considered as a ballpark figure when the actual cost was in excess of $20,000 when the smoke cleared.*

Balls to the wall

Meaning: Giving it every effort you and your equipment have got, without holding back.

Example: *It was 110 in the shade when the '73 Porsche Carrera RSR screamed through the pass, balls to the wall, in the Baja Rally race.*

Bang for (one's) buck

Meaning: Value for your cost.

Example: *When I settled into Business Class on the flight to Japan, I knew that I had gotten the best bang for my buck in booking this trip.*

A bang-up job

Meaning: Excellent work and results.

Example: *For a First Grader, Bobbie Brooks did a bang-up job* *on his longhand letters a-through-p in both capitals and lower-case letters.*

(To) bank on (something)

Meaning: To rely on something with confidence.

Example: *Her father looked the boy in the eye and casually cautioned him, "Be sure to bring Clarice home by 11:00 p.m., or you'll deal with me later, and you can bank on that."*

Barking up the wrong tree

Meaning: Obliviously pursuing the wrong objective, source or person.

Example: *Chris P. Bacon appeared dejected when exiting City Hall, but he had been barking up the wrong tree in his efforts to secure a name change.*

Bark is worse than (someone's) bite

Meaning: The person's menacing demeanor is not reflective of their relatively neutral presence.

Example: *The woman came off as a tough public official, but once we got to know each other, I realized that her bark was clearly worse than her bite.*

Bar none

Meaning: With no exceptions.

Example: *Anyone from Long Beach, California knows that the best ice cream shop, bar none, is Periwinkel's Ice Cream Social over on 2nd Street and Livingston Drive.*

Base on balls

Meaning: An expression in baseball whereby the batter is "awarded" First Base if, prior to hitting the ball into fair territory or striking out, he is pitched, and does not swing at, four non-strike pitches.

Example: *"Lucky-lefty" Louie led the league in base on balls stats with 172 in 482 at-bats.*

Bat an eye

Meaning: Show concern, surprise or distrust.

Example: *The idea was to imply that the classic car could bring over one million dollars at auction, and when nobody batted an eye, we set the Reserve at $1,260,000.*

Batten down the hatches

Meaning: Originally a nautical term, its broader meaning is to take all extra precautions for impending trouble.

Example: *When his furious spouse burst through the barroom door, it was batten down the hatches for Victor Villalobos and his voluptuous concubine Margarita Maldonado.*

Be-all and end-all

Meaning: The ultimate example of something.

Example: *The ecstatic social media influencer, Penelope Switzenheimer, was the be-all and end-all of shuffle dancing.*

Bear a grudge against (someone)

Meaning: Harbor an enduring intention to seek revenge.

Example: *The last thing that the actor needed was bearing a grudge against the insipid casting director.*

Bear fruit
Meaning: Produce results.
Example: *George was hoping against hope that his unique paper airplane designs would "take off" and bear fruit for him.*

Bear (something) in mind
Meaning: Remember to consider.
Example: *If you bear in mind that the threat of imminent force is required for the defense of self-defense to arise, you may want to be more cautious about striking first.*

Beat around the bush
Meaning: To talk or write about something indirectly, without expressly getting to the point.
Example: *William Oppenheimer III was amused when his daughter, Penelope, opted to beat around the bush, instead of asking directly for a Lamborghini Aventador for her 16th birthday present.*

Beat to windward
Meaning: A sailing term for sailing at the highest (that is: *smallest*) angle into the wind which is possible according to the "lift" characteristics of the boat and sail.
Example: *It was salty, wet and cold aboard Pelican's Roost as we beat to windward along the coast of California.*

Beat (someone) to the punch

Meaning: To reveal or accomplish something first, before someone else does.

Example: *The esteemed Mister Winterbottom, Esquire, beat the young prosecutor to the punch when he tactfully revealed, in his Opening Statement to the jury, that his innocent client, Winston Underhill, was a man with a very sordid past.*

Beating a dead horse

Meaning: Describing the same information or argument over and over, *ad nauseam*, despite the fact that there could be no favorable outcome from the diatribe.

Example: *Realizing he was beating a dead horse asking for the snowboarder to ride more cautiously, the Ski Patrolman instead confiscated the guest's Day Pass.*

(To) beat the rap

Meaning: To have a criminal arrest or prosecution dismissed, or to be found Not Guilty.

Example: *Jimmy John Holstein emerged triumphantly from the Courthouse after beating the rap on extortion charges, only to be placed in cuffs by his nemesis, Homicide Detective John C. Rippins, on a murder beef.*

Beauty's in the eye of the beholder

Meaning: Each person has their own version of what constitutes beauty.

Example: *In the* Beauty & the Beast *film, Belle learns to love* *the Beast, proving once and for all that beauty's in the eye of the beholder.*

Beauty's only skin deep

Meaning: A person's beautiful appearance does not assure that they have an honest or otherwise desirable character.

Example: *Several men at Umberto's Senior Center learned the hard way that beauty's only skin deep, when they discovered their bank accounts had been emptied by the lovely octogenarian spinster.*

Be careful what you wish for

Meaning: Poorly thought-out desires can have unexpected bad consequences.

Example: *When June Merriweather was cautioned by several naysayers to be careful what she wished for, she laughed and gleefully purchased yet $300.00 more in Super-Mega Lotto tickets.*

Beggars can't be choosers

Meaning: When asking for aide, one should be flexible in appreciating the kind of aide provided.

Example: *Oliver settled for his neighbor's well-worn, Acme brand basketball, since beggars can't be choosers.*

Beginner's luck

Meaning: Success, by an inexperienced person, attributed for no other rational explanation than to be from pure chance.

Example: *Past Champion Winston Hightower was favored to win the Grocery Checkers Open Championship, but by unmitigated beginners luck, first-year checker Melissa Supinich took top prize, completing her bag with the broccoli in just under 7.37 seconds!*

(To be) behind bars
Meaning: Incarcerated in a lock-down facility.
Example: *While the police officer beat the murder rap, a U.S. Senator landed behind bars following her irresponsible call for mass violence.*

Behind (one's) back
Meaning: Some trusted person secretly acting contrary to one's interests.
Example: *I thought I knew you, but going behind my back and hitting on my girlfriend is way out of line, and I'll warn you right now—stay away from me.*

Behind the eight ball
Meaning: When circumstances have created a tough or dangerous situation for someone.
Example: *The conscientious young lawyer found herself behind the eight ball when her client's blood-alcohol test results came back at .27—over three times the legal limit.*

Bench jockey
Meaning: Largely a baseball term, for players who razz their opponents from the dugout during a baseball game.

Example: *Base Coaches originated from vociferous "bench" players, but in today's game of baseball, dugouts are filled with bench jockeys.*

Bend over backwards

Meaning: Using extra efforts to help resolve a situation.

Example: *Marci was willing to bend over backwards to help her husband, Zittel Zingenhofer, resolve his financial difficulties, but he was arrested on ten Counts of bank embezzlement before she could intervene.*

(Give the) benefit of the doubt

Meaning: Resolve conflicts of interpretation in favor of the accused.

Example: *The jury seemed willing to give defendant Miller the benefit of the doubt, but this all dissolved when Miller exposed himself in open Court during the accuser's testimony on direct examination.*

The best of the best

Meaning: The hyperbole within the hyperbole; the elite best.

Example: *The Chihuahua, Pepe Vargus Caliente, edged out the Standard Poodle, Gerard Pom-pom Incroyable, for the Grand Award as the best of the best.*

The best of both worlds

Meaning: The quality of concurrently achieving key criteria of two widely divergent events or concepts.

Example: *Tottie Tupelo discovered the best of both worlds when the studio exhibited her countryside film outdoors and paid her, to boot, for her appearance fee.*

Better lucky than good

Meaning: At times, it seems that good fortune can be more advantageous than good skills.

Example: *When the Tour professional shanked a shot that hit a tree, bounced on the cart path, careened off a rock and landed in the cup on the fly, he joked to his caddie, "Better lucky than good."*

The better part of

Meaning: More than half of something.

Example: *Wendy let her date wait for her for the better part of fifteen minutes before walking down the stairway to reveal her beautiful Prom outfit and lovely hairstyle.*

Better safe than sorry

Meaning: An extra measure of caution and preparation can guard against problems in the future.

Example: *The Prima Ballerina was better safe than sorry as she tightly griped the handrail of the icy stairway leading to the venue's outdoor parking lot.*

Better than a poke in the eye from a sharp stick

Meaning: It may not be the most fantastic possible outcome, but it's still not too shabby.

Example: *Mister Martingale emerged from the fisticuffs not entirely unscathed, but as Inglenook lay dazed in a puddle of* *mud, Martingale surveyed his own minor injuries and remarked, "It's better than a poke in the eye from a sharp stick," and strolled confidently away.*

Better to give than receive

Meaning: There's a certain ultimate and enduring pleasure derived from giving something of value to another and this often surpasses the joy of receiving something.

Example: *The tired, weathered and hungry homeless-man fed the bulk of the dumpster-scraps to his trusted dog, Fido, since he knew it was better to give than receive.*

Between a rock and a hard place

Meaning: Faced with two equally troublesome options.

Example: *Manuel Ortega found himself between a rock and a hard place when threatened with 20-years in federal prison versus cooperating against the deadly and unforgiving Sinaloa Cartel.*

Beyond a shadow of a doubt

Meaning: Something that is believed to be true beyond any serious question or reservation.

Example: *Virtually all of the protesters believed in his absolute innocence, beyond a shadow of a doubt, but the prosecutor and County Sheriff both held vastly different views of the facts.*

Beyond the pale

Meaning: Entirely outside the scope of acceptable affairs or behavior.

Example: *Interrupting the group training session and loudly* *reprimanding Jethro for not completing college was simply beyond the pale for a competent Supervisor's actions.*

The bigger they are, the harder they fall

Meaning: The more powerful a person or organization, the more difficult it is to recover from a major defeat or disaster.

Example: *Following their CEO's conviction of multiple counts of rape, Retro Film International discovered first-hand the meaning of, "The bigger they are, the harder they fall."*

Bite off more than you can chew

Meaning: Taking on a commitment or activity that exceeds one's capacity to deliver.

Example: *The fledgling actor bit off more than he could chew in a feature film, supporting role audition, after lying about his credits.*

(To) bite the bullet

Meaning: To accept the setback and make adjustments accordingly.

Example: *Acme Explosives had to bite the bullet when premature detonation blew up Wile E. Coyote, and the Road Runner sued for Negligent Infliction of Emotional Distress.*

Bite the dust

Meaning: Experience an unexpected fall or setback.

Example: *The bull-rider bit the dust hard, a mere two-tenths of a second short of the requisite 8-second ride on Grave Robber.*

Bitter pill to swallow

Meaning: A true fact or actual circumstance which is difficult to accept.

Example: *Marvin was devoted to his brilliant girlfriend, Dr. Priscilla Pumpernickel, and her failure to achieve tenure on the second attempt was a bitter pill to swallow.*

Black and blue

Meaning: Bruised physically.

Example: *The young T-ball player was black and blue, but elated in his successful head-first slide into home plate!*

(To) black out

Meaning: Fall into an unconscious state.

Example: *When the renown and sanctimonious speaker spotted two uniformed police officers entering the Middle School auditorium, he paused mid-sentence, took hold of the podium and blacked out.*

A blessing in disguise

Meaning: A benefit underlying an apparent difficulty created by something.

Example: *The accidental breakage of the porcelain dog family heirloom became a blessing in disguise as $3,767 in currency was discovered concealed within.*

Bless your heart

Meaning: An expression of very personal appreciation.

Example: *Young Julie presented her ailing Great Grandmother,*

Abigale Johnson, with a single yellow rose for her 98th Birthday, and Abigale whispered in Julie's ear, "Well bless your heart, Julie, and you should know, you're in my Last Will and Testament big time."

(To be) blind as a bat

Meaning: Either blind or so impaired in sight to be effectively blind.

Example: *Upon being called out on highly questionable strikes, the Yankee's slugger, Peter Finkelstein, turned on the Umpire and screamed, "Why you must be blind as a bat!" whereupon the Umpire ejected Finkelstein from the ballgame.*

Blind date

Meaning: A personal social meetup, typically set up by mutual friends, between two strangers; also, either one of the strangers comprising that blind date.

Example: *Belinda Carmichael listened stoically while her blind date described the mating habits of the Dung Beetle in excruciating detail.*

The blind leading the blind

Meaning: A less-than-capable leader guiding a less-than-capable subordinate.

Example: *It was a classic matter of the blind leading the blind as factory superintendent Mathias offered blatantly mistaken advice to Fred Oosthuizen regarding the operative details of a sophisticated extrusion machine.*

Blind luck

Meaning: A successful explanation or action that is the result of sheer guesswork.

Example: *Mary Snitchelbaum won three Bingo cards that day, but the girls believed it was all blind luck, and they were not amused.*

The blink of an eye

Meaning: An instant; an extremely brief period of time.

Example: *In the blink of an eye, and a solid tap from one of the wheels of its competitor in the Sunset turn at Buttonwillow Raceway, Team Red fell from second to third in class by 8/1,000ths of one second.*

(Can't get) blood from a turnip

Meaning: You'll never collect a debt from an impecunious debtor.

Example: *The "collection specialist" from the mob was well aware of the adage, "You can't get blood from a turnip," but he decided to give the deadbeat special motivation by breaking his left arm in three places.*

Blood is thicker than water

Meaning: Family ties are always stronger than friendships or business alliances.

Example: *The veteran cop released his bank-robber brother from custody, telling him, "I'm cuttin' you a break today, 'cause blood is thicker than water, but don't test my loyalties again."*

Blow off steam

Meaning: Engage in an activity or a tirade to release stress.

Example: *Upon hearing of the impending capital gains tax rate hike, CEO Pendergrass blew off stream by stepping into the stairwell and bellowing, "Sweet-Mary-mother-of-god!"*

Blow the lid off (something)

Meaning: Make a game-changing, major revelation about a dangerous or otherwise controversial situation.

Example: *A Big Pharma competitor, in its zeal to capture more market share, just blew the lid off of the vaccine-safety myth by disclosing an insider report showing that the competitor vaccine death-rate was* far higher *than publicly acknowledged.*

Blow the whistle

Meaning: To inform on someone to higher authorities.

Example: *The obsequious accountant decided to blow the whistle on her employer's rampant securities fraud after the CEO described her derrière as being "grossly obese."*

Blue wall of silence

Meaning: An informal understanding among some law enforcement officers to never inform on their fellow officers for wrong-doing.

Example: *The blue wall of silence held strong as Officer Alonzo Munsterhausen replied, "I can't recall" to every single question pertaining to Officer Briscoe Brinkenhoffer's use-of-force administrative inquiry.*

A bone of contention

Meaning: A principal issue of dispute.

Example: *Without doubt, one bone of contention was whether the transgender athlete had completed the requisite hormone therapy regimen.*

Boots on the ground

Meaning: Soldiers, or any participants for that matter, physically present and available for action.

Example: *The Commander-in-Chief inquired of the Pentagon liaison, "If we choose to invade North Korea, just how many boots on the ground are we talking about?"; to which the wry reply was, "All of them."*

Bore (someone) to death

Meaning: To be painfully tedious and tiresome.

Example: *Belinda was bored to death by her blind date's obsession with Entomology, and politely requested that the date be concluded posthaste.*

Bottom of the ninth

Meaning: The final stage of an undertaking, with the last opportunities for success.

Example: *For the Forbes Fine Silver Company, it was the bottom of the ninth in its dog-eat-dog struggle for market share against the porcelain pot conglomerate.*

Bottoms up

Meaning: A toast for good cheer.

Example: *At precisely 1:59 a.m. in the then-empty dive bar, the plastered drunk held his glass high, fell off the bar stool and from the floor declared, "Bottoms up!"*

Bound and determined

Meaning: Fully committed to do some particular activity.

Example: *Penelope Snodgrass was bound and determined to be the most prolific crochetier in the Petaluma Crochet Society for the entire year.*

Boxed in

Meaning: In a difficult predicament involving multiple adverse forces.

Example: *The coppers thought they had bank robber Ruddy Jenkins all boxed in, but what they didn't know was that a cellar door led to the sewer system, which led to a speedboat waiting for him less than one mile away.*

Boys will be boys

Meaning: Sometimes men engage in rowdy or foolish behavior.

Example: *The wives sat calmly on the covered porch, drinking banana daquiris, as the men proved once again that boys will be boys, playing flag football in the mud during a rain storm.*

Bread always falls butter-side down

Meaning: Given the chance, the worst will occur.

Example: *As the handsome young man whispered in her ear,*

"Your boyfriend will never know," the girl pulled away, knowing that bread always falls butter-side down.

Bread and butter

Meaning: The essential basics of something.

Example: *Dishing out speed-trap citations was the bread and butter of Cornville, Arizona's one-man Sheriff's Office.*

Break a leg

Meaning: In the acting profession, an expression of good luck.

Example: *As the young man left the house for his Cheerios audition, his loving mother gave him a kiss on the cheek and told him, "Break a leg, Jack; love you."*

Break out in a cold sweat

Meaning: To sweat rapidly and profusely in reaction to sudden stress.

Example: *Two-time loser Mikey Moran was typically cool as a cucumber, but when the coppers flashed the incriminating photo to him, he broke out in a cold sweat and confessed to the Grand Theft Auto charge.*

Break the bank

Meaning: It is so expensive that it's a game-changer in the sense of costing more than can be afforded; often stated in the negative.

Example: *Tyrone Jones had six mouths to feed at home, but* *with his second job, buying a new Chevy Camaro wouldn't break the bank.*

Break the ice

Meaning: Doing or saying something in order to casually commence a discussion or interaction.

Example: *President Trump decided to break the ice with the North Korean dictator by offering to have their meeting take place at a karaoke bar in downtown Tokyo.*

Breathe easy/easier

Meaning: Relaxing to an extent, following the occurrence of something favorable.

Example: *Elise Bunberry was finally able to breathe easy when her principal competitor, Irene Toppelman, fell five hot dogs and buns behind with only 30 seconds remaining in the County Fair contest.*

Breathing down (someone's) neck

Meaning: Closely observing, monitoring or investigating someone's activities.

Example: *With Professor Binderlaut breathing down his neck, Billy Tinderhooper was unable to cheat in the Social Studies final exam.*

Breath of fresh air

Meaning: Something said or done which was a break from the dogma and tedium of prior events.

Example: *The substitute director's relaxed attitude with both cast and crew was a breath of fresh air from the tyrannical oppression exhibited by her ousted predecessor.*

(To) bring (someone) to

Meaning: To aide in restoring an unconscious person back to consciousness.

Example: *A Medic stepped in to bring the stunt man to, following the horrific motorcycle stunt accident.*

Bring to a head

Meaning: Cause something to now resolve one way or the other.

Example: *The Moot Court Judge vehemently interjected, "Miss Edgerton, please bring your argument to a head on the issue of the warrantless border search of the laptop computer!"*

Broad in the beam

Meaning: Obese, particularly in the backside.

Example: *The sailor's bride was broad in the beam, but otherwise delightfully attractive.*

A broken plate does not mend

Meaning: Some things which are done, cannot be undone.

Example: *Despite the chronic abuser's pleas for forgiveness, and with only her dignity and future intact, the battered girl walked out of his front door and commented, "A broken plate does not mend."*

Brownie points

Meaning: A somewhat tongue-in-cheek, or even derogatory, manner of describing recognition of achievements.

Example: *My job in representing unvaccinated teachers at the District regarding the vaccine Mandate is to find ways to help them retain their jobs, if only in remote-working situations, not to accumulate Brownie points for being an outspoken attorney on the irrationality of the vaccine mandate itself.*

A bull in a China shop

Meaning: Used as a metaphor for being awkward, clumsy and prone to accidentally breaking things.

Example: *The contumacious youth was a bull in a china shop as he bumped into or knocked over display after display in the gas station mini-mart.*

Bundle of nerves

Meaning: Stressed out.

Example: *Walking through Customs at LAX, the Columbian mother of three was a bundle of nerves, and for good reason.*

Business as usual

Meaning: Adhering to the status quo in actions.

Example: *After cordially greeting the public, it was business as usual as the marginally competent Traffic Commissioner proceeded to hand out Guilty verdicts left and right.*

The business end (of something)

    Meaning: The functional end of a tool or instrument, such as the end of a firearm from which a bullet is fired.

    Example: *The cowardly perpetrator repeatedly struck the helpless Chinese woman with the business end of a baseball bat.*

A busman's holiday

    Meaning: Doing on holiday what is done at one's job.

    Example: *In a busman's holiday, the ocean beach lifeguard spent his one day off lounging on the sand with his sumptuous girlfriend.*

Butt dial

    Meaning: The process of inadvertently instructing one's mobile phone, through accidental touch commands typically while the phone is in a pocket of one's clothing, to connect with another phone number.

    Example: *One excellent reason to delete contacts from your cell phone once you decide to never talk to them again, is the risk of butt dialing one and becoming trapped in an uncomfortable conversation.*

Butter (someone) up

    Meaning: Compliment someone to make them vulnerable to persuasion.

    Example: *The Officer proceeded to butter up the Police Chief once the missing bodycam evidence surfaced online.*

Buy the farm

Meaning: To die.

Example: *The old coot bought the farm after all, but what a way to go with Spinster Mary Jean Merriweather.*

By and by

Meaning: As time passes.

Example: *I knew that my sister Caroline would learn to care for me again by and by, despite our past misgivings.*

By the skin of (one's) teeth

Meaning: Just enough to barely accomplish something.

Example: *After a grueling, 6-hour endurance race, Team Red won the Spec Miata class by the skin of its teeth.*

Cake-walk

Meaning: Something that is not a problem, since it's an easy task or challenge.

Example: *Marion was very flustered with what she could and could not do in her rehabilitation, but was pleasantly relieved to discover that the flutter kicks were a cake-walk after all.*

Call a spade a spade

Meaning: Describe something directly for what it is, without using a euphemism or beating around the bush.

Example: *Out of season, when you mistake a Doe for a Buck, call a spade a spade—you screwed up royally.*

(To get) called on the carpet

Meaning: To be remonstrated for perceived wrongdoing or incompetence.

Example: *The timing was unfortunate but on her 25th birthday, Nurse Becker was called on the carpet by the fatuous hospital administrator.*

Call dibs

Meaning: To verbally claim priority to something versus other potential claimants.

Example: *When Jimmy Smithers called dibs on shotgun, Craig Peterson sulked into the back seat of the Candy Apple Red, 1952 Chevrolet 2-door sedan.*

Call it a day

Meaning: To finish the activity for at least the time being.

Example: *As the blazing sun dipped below the horizon, Ben Reynolds and his capable son, Ian, decided to call it a day on their backyard, DIY "floating" redwood deck project.*

Call off the dogs

Meaning: Discontinue disparaging remarks against another.

Example: *The warehouse super called off the dogs, after the V.P. of Human Resources warned him about sexual harassment of Marcie Zinderhooper in the shipping department.*

Call shotgun

Meaning: In a situation where three or more persons will be riding in a car, to verbally claim the right to sit in the front window-seat directly opposite the driver.

Example: *Immediately after stepping out of the pizza parlor, Skippy Schuler called shotgun, much to the dismay of Riley and Scooter who were destined, again, to sit in the back seat of Rory's 1952 blue and white Chevy coupe.*

Call the shots

Meaning: Make the major decisions.

Example: *As the undisputed ringleader of this inauspicious band of bank robbers, Yancy Severson called the shots leading to their capture on prime-time national television.*

Call time

Meaning: The time on a particular day when a cast or crew member is to arrive on the set of a production.

Example: *Although his call time wasn't until 5:00 p.m., actor Jack Forbes preferred to be 30 minutes or so early, to account for any unexpected delays.*

The calm before the storm

Meaning: An uneventful period of time preceding the real threat or calamity.

Example: *When the lady of the house returned from work and stepped into the great room, her relaxed demeanor was simply the calm before the storm considering that the family dog, Tiffany, had torn up and completely destroyed their Arizona Leather, 8-foot couch.*

A can of corn

Meaning: A routine fly ball to an outfielder in baseball; an easy task.

Example: *The Hedgehogs lost in the bottom of the Ninth when a pinch hitter for their Closer served up a can of corn to the Jack Rabbit's Center Fielder, for the third and final out.*

A can of worms

Meaning: An event or circumstance fraught with a myriad of adverse complications.

Example: *Contract discussions with the unscrupulous casting director became a can of worms, since she had already lied to the actor about the Best of Show rate.*

Can't get a word in edgewise

Meaning: Unable to contribute to a conversation because of the overly-talkative manner of one of the participants.

Example: *Once Sharon started in about how fabulous her boyfriend Gilbert was, Victoria just couldn't get a word in edgewise and found herself drifting away from the coterie.*

Can't hack it

Meaning: Unable to endure or master something.

Example: *Your incompetence is so frustrating to me and I just can't hack it that you can't hack it.*

Can't/don't hold a candle to (something)

Meaning: Unable to successfully compete with something.

Example: *Carley was a superb swimmer, but couldn't hold a candle to Stephanie Simmersaker in the 200 I.M..*

Can't see the forest from the trees

Meaning: Someone so focused on detail that the overall circumstance is not well understood.

Example: *The Governor couldn't see the forest from the trees when he enabled rampant rapes by allowing male prisoners to* *"identify" as females and then be transferred to incarcerated female populations.*

Cards stacked against (someone)

Meaning: A set of circumstances making an activity much more difficult for someone.

Example: *Personally, I try not to judge someone by their successes or failures, since you never really know if the cards have been stacked against them in life.*

Card up (someone's) sleeve

Meaning: A hidden asset or advantage.

Example: *The savvy politician walked into the hearing as an underdog, but the card up his sleeve was the testimony of an expert who had warned the pharmaceutical industry of the very adverse effects which had been killing people for the past six months.*

Carrot and stick

Meaning: The incentive of a benefit and the extortion of imminent harm.

Example: *As a carrot and stick for the controversial inoculation, the State first offered lottery tickets for those who capitulated to the jab, and then threatened second-class citizenship to those who continued to refuse to risk death and disability.*

Carry the day

Meaning: Push toward victory.

Example: *75-year-old Reginald Smith carried the day for the*

4 by 100-meter swimming relay in the 75-79 age group Master's event, by swimming the anchor leg in a split of 1:10.23.

Case in point

Meaning: An example of the situation described.

Example: *One never knows when danger will present itself and a perfect case in point is the recent report of a Great White Shark literally jumping onto the stern deck of a powerboat off of Catalina Island.*

Cast iron stomach

Meaning: A person's gut which can digest almost all food and drink without the person becoming sick.

Example: *Without doubt, Matt needed a cast iron stomach to eat the spicy hot meals prepared by his Thai mother.*

(To) catch a lot of flak

Meaning: To receive substantial criticism for some action.

Example: *The hapless Home Plate Umpire caught a lot of flak from both managers when he flip-flopped on his Catcher interference call three times!*

Catch as catch can

Meaning: To take, utilize and be satisfied with whatever may be available at the time, without being particularly choosy.

Example: *It was catch as catch can for the drunk 16-year-old high school student when most of the cute girls had already left the school dance for after-parties.*

Catch some z's

Meaning: Get some sleep.

Example: *Relaxing in his trailer, stuntman Zach Underhill decided to catch some z's before his 70-foot high-fall stunt.*

(To) catch the/my drift

Meaning: To understand the overall, general meaning of a statement or conversation.

Example: *I finally caught the drift of Professor Zumwalt's explanation, despite his rambling, virtually incoherent speaking habits.*

Catch your/my death of cold

Meaning: Typically, in inclement weather, to be at risk of becoming sick.

Example: *On my way out the door that night, my Southern auntie handed me a woolen neck-scarf and told me, "Stay safe, Jackie, and don't catch your death of cold."*

(Has the) cat got your tongue?

Meaning: Often a rhetorical comment asking, in effect, "Don't you have anything to say, now?"

Example: *Observing the burglar protruding half-way out of the jewelry store roof, Officer Smedley asked the man, "Good morning to ya, and whatcha doin' there sir, or has the cat got your tongue?"*

Cat nap

Meaning: Sleeping for only a short time during normal

waking hours.

Example: *If I happen to sleep more than a thirty-minute cat nap during the day, I definitely feel "off."*

Caught between the Devil and the deep blue sea

Meaning: At loggerheads in a predicament where both choices are equally terrible.

Example: *With the SEC breathing down his neck, and his "investors" clamoring to recover their life-savings, financial fraudster Hedley Rickenbacker was caught between the Devil and the deep blue sea.*

Caught inside

Meaning: In surfing, when a surfer has not yet completed his paddle out beyond the break and is impacted by white-water ("soup") from the breaking waves.

Example: *Seriously near-sighted Jim Mitchell almost drowned at the Ventura Overhead when he was caught inside by a humongous cleanup set.*

Caught red-handed

Meaning: Discovered either in the act of committing a wrongdoing, or in possession of obviously incriminating evidence of the wrongdoing.

Example: *The hapless culprit was caught red-handed by his mother as he stashed the stolen bicycle in their garage.*

Caught with (one's) hands in the cookie jar

Meaning: Observed stealing.

Example: *The Chief Financial Officer of GMZB Enterprises was caught with her hands in the cookie jar and was summarily placed on unpaid leave pending a full investigation of the fact and extent of the suspected embezzlement.*

Caught with (one's) pants down

Meaning: Something occurred and was detected which constituted an embarrassing revelation about them or an indication of a shortfall in their abilities.

Example: *Attorney Bill Usterhozen was caught with his pants down when it was discovered that his law school was not Harvard, as indicated in his bio, but the unaccredited online school known as Harford School of Law.*

A chain's only as strong as its weakest link

Meaning: A team of people or a series of inter-dependent actions or mechanical steps are only as effective as the least capable and reliable person, action or step.

Example: *Unfortunately for the Billings Hardware softball team, a chain's only as strong as its weakest link, and Winston Pennypacker's failure to get a single hit cost them the Championship.*

Chances are

Meaning: Factors pertaining to the likelihood of this, tip towards the affirmative.

Example: *With a DUI-refusal arrest, chances are the case will go to trial and Guilty Verdicts will be returned.*

Change your tune

Meaning: Adopt a new perspective on a subject.

Example: *The perpetrator quickly changed his tune and copped to the 4-5-9 when the Detectives pointed out he was wearing a distinctive gold watch stolen in the burglary itself.*

Chapter and verse

Meaning: The substance of something in writing.

Example: *Pastor Mueller quoted chapter and verse from the Bible but the young man responded that he didn't believe that ancient book of stories was a credible source of history.*

Charley horse

Meaning: A severe muscle cramp.

Example: *During the first quarter of the State High School Finals water polo game, point-man Charlie Tinkerton had to be substituted out when he developed an excruciatingly painful charley horse in his right hamstring muscle.*

Chase rainbows

Meaning: Pursue one's dreams unapologetically.

Example: *The young black man admitted to chasing rainbows in his desire to become a well-known film star, but his honest passion was enough to avert criticism for the obvious quest for fame and fortune.*

Chase your tail

Meaning: Making a lot of effort but accomplishing nothing.

Example: *The young police officer was chasing her tail in trying to get drugs off the street, and despite her efforts, another youthful seller popped up every time she made one of her sporadic arrests.*

Cheap shot

Meaning: An unsportsmanlike hit or play.

Example: *In the five-round MMA Welter Weight Championship, Tommy was DQ'd for taking a cheap shot at Sanders after the third-round bell.*

Cheat death

Meaning: In some manner, to narrowly avert being killed.

Example: *The tow-in surfer at Jaws cheated death in a spectacular wipeout where despite his inflatable vest he was held under water for nearly a full minute before popping up to the surface.*

Check mate

Meaning: The final, unstoppable move to secure victory.

Example: *It was check mate and game over when the prosecution's final witness pointed, in open Court, to a ring on the defendant's finger and exclaimed, "And that's my husband's ring, with the initials 'JW' on the inside band!"*

The check's in the mail

Meaning: A sarcastic way of stating that some payment is *not* actually going to happen.

Example: *When the disgruntled ex-boyfriend demanded return* *of his $10,000 cash gift, the sumptuous Felicity Smithers laughed as she replied, "Sure thing, Freddie, the check's in the mail."*

Cherry pick

Meaning: Selectively choose items or persons in order to fit your personal purposes.

Example: *The traffic cop, known within the court system as The Machine, inflated his traffic infraction stats by cherry picking locations, in order to issue hundreds of citations for insignificant violations every week.*

Chew the fat

Meaning: Idle conversation.

Example: *Renown criminal defense attorney Priscilla Abernathy was captivated in chewing the fat with the iconic cat burglar, Luther Cross.*

A chicken in every pot

Meaning: A hypothetical something useful and valuable for everyone.

Example: *The cagey politician knew full-well that to garner votes among his constituents "of color," he would need to offer some manner of the proverbial chicken in every pot.*

Chin music

Meaning: In baseball, a pitch thrown high and tight to the batter, causing him to rapidly lean backwards to avoid being struck above his mid-torso.

Example: *With Salgado crowding the plate, southpaw Bill*

Hinkelsteiner served up chin music to put him in his place.

Chip off the old block
Meaning: Highly similar to one's father.
Example: *Clearly a chip off the old block, Petey Pfister was a natural in his father's sport of darts.*

Chip on (one's) shoulder
Meaning: A negative attitude and sense that life is stacked against oneself, marked by aggression.
Example: *Norberg will never forget the day his father accused him of having a chip on his shoulder, and he'll never forgive him for making that uncalled for and hurtful accusation.*

Chock-full
Meaning: An abundance.
Example: *The Louisiana State Fair was chock-full of scantily clad Southern girls dressed in Levi cut-off shorts and skimpy halter tops.*

(To be) chomping at the bit
Meaning: Exceptionally eager.
Example: *The gregarious Navy Seal recruits were chomping at the bit to hit the water for their one-mile, morning swim.*

Circle the wagons
Meaning: To tighten up one's friends, co-workers and resources as a unified force to embolden one's defenses.
Example: *When City of Lancaster sponsored an Antelope*

Valley Fair pie eating contest, City of Palmdale circled the
wagons to promote a hot dog eating contest for the same Antelope
Valley Fair.

Class act

Meaning: An honorable and well-meaning person.
Example: *There's no doubt Sara's boyfriend is a class act, and*
coming to the rescue of her girlfriend at the party was simply one
example of his integrity and compassion.

Clean as a whistle

Meaning: Spotless and free from dirt and stains.
Example: *The barracks latrine was clean as a whistle as Private*
First-Class Roger Rundle proudly completed his afternoon task.

Clean bill of health

Meaning: A doctor's advisement that a person is not sick in
any manner.
Example: *With the esophageal cancer now in full remission,*
Doctor Wellington happily gave my 90-year old father a clean bill
of health.

Cleaned out

Meaning: To remove everything from a particular
container or account.
Example: *The day prior to filing her Dissolution of Marriage*
Petition, Marcy Spindlemeister cleaned out their jointly-held
checking and savings accounts.

Clean hands

    Meaning: Free from deception and illegal conduct.

    Example: *The integrity of the badminton Doubles match was subverted by the players' decision to split the first two games and fight it out in the third, but the technical officials indisputably had clean hands.*

Clean slate

    Meaning: Commencing with reference to neither past conduct nor results.

    Example: *Ted's boss magnanimously offered to continue Ted's employment with a clean slate, but the disgraced shop superintendent opted to quit instead and to find new employment elsewhere.*

Clean sweep

    Meaning: A victory of all of the contests within a particular category.

    Example: *The Red Rock Rovers celebrated their clean sweep over the Pinehurst Pinions by meeting at the local pizza parlor for a rousing lunch.*

Clean (someone's) clock

    Meaning: Beat up someone.

    Example: *Jimmy's father, Manny, stepped in to protect his son from a beating, but the 17-year-old attacker unceremoniously cleaned Manny's clock.*

A cleanup set

Meaning: In surfing, a group of waves that are so much bigger than the typical waves of that session that the largest ones actually break onto the surfers "caught inside" who are trying to paddle to outside the break.

Example: *At least fifteen surfers dove for deep water when a huge cleanup set rolled through at Banzai Pipeline.*

Cleared the benches

Meaning: In baseball, an event causing all of the players from each of the two teams to pour onto the field to fight the opposing team or to defend their teammates.

Example: *Drilling the Pitcher in the back with a 97 miles-per-hour fastball cleared the benches, as a full-scale brawl broke out between the Lancaster Mules and the Bakersfield Badgers.*

Clear the decks

Meaning: Getting unnecessary people or things away from danger.

Example: *In anticipation of the massive hurricane's landfall, Mister Bigelow instructed his property manager to clear the decks of all unsheltered motor vehicles on the estate.*

Close, but no cigar

Meaning: Almost enough, but not quite.

Example: *It was close, but no cigar as Charlie tried to kiss Julie goodnight following the annual Pajama Jump dance, and she shook his hand instead, stating, "Thank you for the fun date."*

A close call

Meaning: A near miss.

Example: *To calm herself, 16-year-old Monica Wellington pulled her father's 1973 Porsche Carrera RS to the curb following the close call with an out-of-control drunk driver.*

Closed book

Meaning: A situation and the resolution thereof which is no longer up for discussion or modification.

Example: *Discussion of where to go on the family camping trip was now a closed book—they were headed for Zermatt, Switzerland for three weeks of skiing!*

Close quarters

Meaning: A lot of people in too small of a space.

Example: *Thousands of unaccompanied migrant children were living in close quarters, in cages for months, before gradually being placed with volunteer families.*

(To) close ranks

Meaning: To present a unified front among allies.

Example: *Faced with mounting administrative pressure for all players to receive the controversial inoculation against the Ebola virus, the footballers closed ranks. threatening to strike if any such mandate were implemented.*

Close shave

Meaning: Narrowly avoiding injury.

Example: *Table tennis guru Okijima Tanaka had a close shave—when diving for a backhand smash, his shoes lost traction and he narrowly missed clipping the table with his forehead.*

Cloud of suspicion

Meaning: Vague allegations and assertions of wrongdoing, without any actual and reliable proof.

Example: *Cornelius Uppenpfeiffer was the obvious favorite for the office of Class President of Paramount High School, but the cloud of suspicion concerning his suspected (though denied) obsession with Neapolitan ice cream, topped with yellow mustard, could have an adverse impact.*

Coast is clear

Meaning: The danger has passed, or at least has not yet arrived.

Example: *The getaway driver quietly announced that the coast was clear, whereupon Monty instructed the demolition crew to begin burning through the bank vault door.*

Cock and bull story

Meaning: A detailed lie.

Example: *Abigail Osterhaven spun her cock and bull story to the jury for well over an hour, but within twenty-five minutes of deliberations, a verdict of Guilty was returned on each of seven Counts of felony Welfare Fraud.*

Cold as a frosted frog

Meaning: Very cold weather.

Example: *Wilbur was cold as a frosted frog as he sat fishing on Lake Winnipego in the dead of winter.*

Cold feet

Meaning: Reluctance to act due to insidious fear.

Example: *The informant understandably had cold feet about wearing a wire, considering that he would be meeting with the DeNiro Family mob's most notorious enforcer, Jimmy "Two Eyes" Maldonado.*

Colder than a well-digger's ass

Meaning: Very cold weather.

Example: *When the youngster commented that it was "colder than a well-digger's ass," the seasoned cowboy slowed his horse, glanced over at his son and laughed.*

Cold hands, warm heart

Meaning: A superstition that a person with physically cold hands often has a kind and caring persona.

Example: *As she gently held her fiancé's hands, Eleanor Pickleberry softly cooed, "Cold hands, warm heart."*

(To give someone) the cold shoulder

Meaning: To purposefully ignore someone.

Example: *Now that Myrtle Penstermaeker had inherited a cool million from her long-lost uncle, she gave the cold shoulder to her ailing husband, Viktor.*

Cold turkey

Meaning: Cessation without any ameliorating therapy or medication.

Example: *Stanley confronted his personal obsession with jelly beans by opting to quit cold turkey.*

Collect dust

Meaning: Continue in disuse.

Example: *My baseball glove was collecting dust in the closet until I met this really cool girl who played a lot of softball in high school, and so now my glove is still in the closet.*

(To) come clean

Meaning: To tell the truth and reveal incriminating facts and detail.

Example: *The veteran copper implored the young hooligan to come clean about the armored car heist, but the miscreant instead invoked the Fifth.*

Come on the heels of (something)

Meaning: To follow something closely in sequence.

Example: *Indictment of several Big Pharma officers and directors came hard on the heels of the discovery of foreign particles of a metallic substance in most vials of the controversial injection.*

Come out fighting/swinging

Meaning: To enter a situation with an aggressive action.

Example: *The Affinity Plus marketing team decided to come* *out fighting when presenting their proposed limerick-based ad campaign to their Irish beer brewery.*

Come out of the woodwork

Meaning: A lot of this all over the place.

Example: *Once we arrived in Thailand, hot girls were coming out of the woodwork and all of them seemed to like American guys.*

Come rain or shine

Meaning: Regularly, regardless of adverse circumstances.

Example: *Preparing for the race, Jordan was up at 5:30 a.m. every day, come rain or shine, for a seven-mile run.*

Comes with the territory

Meaning: Something that is indelibly linked to something else.

Example: *Once I met Julia, I learned all about the latest soap opera plots, since it comes with the territory in dating this girl.*

Come to grips

Meaning: Learn to understand and accept something.

Example: *After the shark bite, Chris had to come to grips with the real possibility of death in the ocean.*

Coming out

Meaning: To reveal oneself as gay or lesbian.

Example: *In revealing his coming out, his toughest audience was his wife.*

Comparing apples to/and oranges

Meaning: The logical error of trying to make a direct comparison between persons, things or situations which have substantially different and distinguishable main components.

Example: *Referencing federal procedure in a State court civil proceeding was comparing apples to oranges.*

Connect the dots

Meaning: Putting together the facts to arrive at a conclusion.

Example: *Connecting the dots was the easy part and deciding what I could do about this national disaster was the real challenge.*

A contract of adhesion

Meaning: A legal term describing a (typically, written) agreement, the essential terms of which are dictated by the stronger party and are non-negotiable.

Example: *Judge Learned Hand strictly construed the arbitration clause, wisely holding that it was contained within a contract of adhesion.*

(To) cook the books

Meaning: To willfully alter accounting records to hide nefarious transactions.

Example: *The gay lawyer, Will Ted Flower, willfully assisted his guilty-as-sin client in cooking the books in order to defend the tax fraud prosecution.*

Cool as a cucumber

Meaning: To be uncommonly calm under pressure or stress.

Example: *Beatrice Keister was cool a cucumber, as she blasted the home-invasion intruders with the business end of her Winchester pump, 12-guage shotgun.*

Cool (one's) heels

Meaning: Take a break.

Example: *Following my near-collision on the mountain highway, I decided to cool my heels for an hour to think about the potential ramifications of my conduct.*

Cop a plea

Meaning: Plead guilty, typically with a "plea bargain" in place.

Example: *Mario pleaded with his Court-appointed lawyer to take the case to trial, but the lawyer saw the writing on the wall and persuaded Mario to cop a plea and start his bullet in County.*

(To) cost (one) an arm and a leg

Meaning: To be overly expensive in either money or in other, less tangible, ways.

Example: *The I-phone cost the impecunious thespian an arm and a leg, but it was well worth the expense considering the digital-quality requirements of her self-tape auditions.*

A couch potato

Meaning: A person who spends an inordinate amount of time in sedentary activities at home.

Example: *Jack's friend Bob was a notorious couch potato during the entirety of the NFL season.*

Country mile

Meaning: A very long distance in the particular circumstances.

Example: *Wide Receiver Bruster Hollandale had to run a country mile for that pass, but his spectacular catch in the End Zone left his Titans with only a 3-point deficit at the Half.*

Cover-to-cover

Meaning: The contents of the entire book from start to finish.

Example: *When speaking with Mickey, I thanked him for sending over his script and assured him that not only did I read it cover-to-cover, but that I enjoyed it a lot!*

(To) cover your/my tracks

Meaning: To deliberately disguise one's actions.

Example: *The lawyer was not inclined to directly advise his client to cover his tracks, but he did mention in passing that should the police arrive with a warrant in hand, they couldn't seize what was no longer present in the structure.*

A coward dies a thousand deaths

Meaning: The aftermath of fear and timidity is a measure of its own punishment.

Example: *A fallen hero dies but once, while a coward dies a thousand deaths of shame.*

Cowboy/man up

Meaning: Show some courage and get the job done.

Example: *Willie was still sore from head to toe from the beatdown he got at the docks yesterday, but he had bills to pay and needed to cowboy up and report for work.*

Crack of dawn

Meaning: When the sky to the east begins to have sunlight, prior to actual sunrise.

Example: *At the crack of dawn, the yacht* Funtastic *headed to the shoals for a day of fishing.*

Crack the case

Meaning: Discover the key evidence in a criminal investigation to prove the case against someone.

Example: *Undertaking DNA analysis on relatives of each of several suspects allowed investigators to crack the case of the Golden State Killer.*

The cream of the crop

Meaning: The best of the lot.

Example: *By pure, unmitigated happenstance, the freshman walk-on turned out to be the cream of the crop in defensive skills at Third Base.*

Cream rises to the top

Meaning: Quality, character, personality or solid work habits naturally result in success and recognition.

Example: *Irene's uncanny archery skills were proof-positive that cream rises to the top, considering that her first draw was less than one month ago.*

Crime doesn't pay

Meaning: In the long-run, the adverse consequences from criminal conduct will outweigh any benefits.

Example: *Convicted residential, serial burglar, Reynoso Cabrillo, had the next 15-years in a Texas State Prison to contemplate that crime doesn't pay.*

Critical mass

Meaning: The greater weight of the evidence, argument or political movement.

Example: *Critical mass of the "My body, my choice" movement regarding the COVID-19 vaccines was the unification of black Democrats and all Republicans against the efficacy and safety of the vaccines.*

Cross that bridge when (one) comes to it

Meaning: Deal with an important issue later, when it becomes the issue needing immediate attention.

Example: *The nefarious trio was uncertain as to exactly how to fence the distinctive jewels after the robbery, but decided to cross that bridge when (and if) they came to it.*

Cross the line

Meaning: To act in a manner contrary to established limits acceptable to one's group.

Example: *Bruno knew full well that he had crossed the line by roughly laying hands on Quinn's old-lady, and was prepared to accept the consequences of a severe beat-down.*

Curiosity killed the cat

Meaning: Poking your nose into other people's affairs can easily result in trouble.

Example: *Pete "Notorious" Abernathy's girlfriend wondered where all the suitcases of cash came from, but she steered clear of his "business" affairs, understanding that curiosity killed the cat.*

The customer's always right

Meaning: A retailer's policy of coddling, and generally giving the benefit of the doubt to, customers as a means of promoting good will and future business.

Example: *The shift-supervisor happily accepted return of the tennis shoes and authorized a full cash refund despite some wear on the shoes, since the customer's always right and the product loss was negligible.*

Cut/make a long story short

Meaning: To generally summarize a long, involved situation to make it fit into a shorter conversation.

Example: *To cut a long story short, I was present at the concert in Las Vegas when the shooting began, and in the melee, I ran for cover to the interior of a nearby food truck.*

Cut and run

> **Meaning:** Leave a job, situation or event precipitously and without warning.
>
> **Example:** *The cowardly perpetrator decided to cut and run for Mexico rather than to face the music for his despicable double-murder.*

Cut corners

> **Meaning:** To utilize shortcuts, sometimes at the expense of quality or effectiveness, in order to complete a project in less time or expense.
>
> **Example:** *Matilda Miller was let go when it was determined she had cut corners one-too-many times in her bookkeeping entries, resulting in a minor accounting catastrophe.*

Cute as the Dickens

> **Meaning:** Very sweet and attractive small child, girl or female.
>
> **Example:** *With a pink bow in her hair, and a lavender party dress, young Priscilla Jenkins was definitely cute as the Dickens.*

Cut (one's) losses

> **Meaning:** Get out of a bad situation, having suffered some damage or loss, but eliminating further, future loss potential.
>
> **Example:** *Peterson decided to cut his losses and unload his inoperable classic-motorcycle on the cheap rather than invest another $5,000 in an engine rebuild.*

Cut (someone) some slack

    Meaning: Let up on the pressure.

    Example: *Sherry's supervisor advised her to cut Thomas some slack considering that he had only recently returned to work following a 30-day leave of absence due to job-related stress.*

Cut the mustard

    Meaning: Meet the needs for the task.

    Example: *There was no doubt as to the educational background of the new teacher, and whether he could cut the mustard with an inner-city high school class was the real issue.*

Cut ties

    Meaning: To disconnect or otherwise distance oneself from another person or organization.

    Example: *Once numerous scandalous accusations were made against the film producer, action superstar Jimmy "The Amazing One" Jameson cut ties, announcing that he would never work with that rapist again.*

Cutting edge

    Meaning: At the forefront of the applicable technology.

    Example: *Jack used cutting edge legal research tools to research and craft a memo regarding the limitations of the pre-nuptial agreement entered into by his new client.*

Cut to the chase

    Meaning: Get to the central point of the lecture or discussion.

Example: *As the first-year law student droned on about the facts of Palsgraf versus Long Island Railroad Company, Professor Marshal Uppenwager interrupted, stating, "Excuse me, Miss Nuggles, cut to the chase, please."*

D

Damaged goods

Meaning: A person who has been so harmed by adverse personal experiences during their lifetime that their judgment, attitude and actions have been irreparably impaired.

Example: *Sadly, a lot of the troubled kids we see in Juvenile Court are being raised by parents who are themselves damaged goods.*

Dark horse

Meaning: A long-shot for the win, but unexpectedly succeeding.

Example: *The thing about my dad was that he was a dark horse, a sort of casual, laid-back dark horse, and almost nobody knew how fabulously successful he was in business.*

Days are numbered

Meaning: Someone or something will end soon, one way or another.

Example: *Considering how infrequently I've been on commercial auditions lately, the days are numbered for XYZ Talent Agency representing me commercially.*

Dead air

Meaning: In the course of a broadcast, where there is an interruption in the signal.

Example: *The worst possible outcome came to fruition when just as the baseball game was about to end, we had a fifteen-minute period of dead air.*

Dead as a doornail

Meaning: Obviously, completely and absolutely dead.

Example: *When that wiener-dog appeared at a full run from in front of the speeding car to my left, it never made it past my car and was dead as a doornail by the time it landed off to the side of the road.*

Dead even

Meaning: Tie score.

Example: *At the end of regulation time, the score in this Juniors ice hockey match, was dead even.*

A dead duck

Meaning: Someone or something who is either defeated or dead, or is about to become defeated or dead.

Example: *The rodeo clown was a dead duck once he tripped and the bull, Grievous Error, was bearing down on him rapidly.*

Dead heat

Meaning: Absolutely even at the finish line.

Example: *Even after examining the photo-finish photography, the two greyhounds finished in a dead heat, and first place was awarded to them both.*

Dead in the water

Meaning: All forward progress in an activity has come to a halt.

Example: *Once the Baltimore Bombers had used up their last pitcher in the extra-innings marathon, they were dead in the water and gave up five consecutive dingers.*

Dead meat

Meaning: In deep, deep trouble and at risk for serious consequences.

Example: *About that dirt-bag who stole my mobile phone—he's gonna be dead meat when I put my hands on him.*

Dead men tell no tales

Meaning: An expression often attributed to pirate jargon—a dead witness cannot testify.

Example: *Crime boss Timothy Nolan knew that his second-in-command, Brian O'Flaherty, had been flipped, but he also knew that dead men tell no tales.*

The dead of night

Meaning: So late, even the toads are quiet.

Example: *He almost literally drug himself up the stairway to his dilapidated apartment in the dead of night, hoping beyond hope that his nearly-late paper on the meaning of the Genesis chapter in the Bible would be accepted without penalty.*

The dead of winter

Meaning: Within the coldest part of the winter months.

Example: *The epic thriller,* White Out!, *had been lensed in the Colorado Rockies in the dead of winter.*

Dead right

Meaning: Absolutely correct.

Example: *Private Eye Summerland Winters was dead right in his deduction as to the whereabouts of the body, but now the question became—Who is she?*

Dead set

Meaning: Fully committed to a decision.

Example: *Jack was so over studying all waking hours that he was dead set on surfing Trestles, Saturday morning.*

Dead tired

Meaning: Exceptionally exhausted.

Example: *After three hours and five complete matches of fast-paced doubles badminton, Shirley Chen was dead tired and decided that enough was enough.*

Dead to rights

Meaning: Caught or detected, in a crime or other

wrongdoing, beyond reasonable dispute.

Example: *The F.B.I. had the notorious Billy Finkelstein dead to rights when they executed a federal search warrant and seized a printing press, plates for $100 U.S. currency and over $200,000 in funny money.*

Dead wrong

Meaning: Absolutely incorrect.

Example: *When little Scottie Hauser answered the math question in front of his Third-Grade class, he strongly suspected that he was dead wrong in the computation, but stood proud and resolute with the fact that he had given any answer at all.*

Deaf as a post

Meaning: Completely or functionally deaf in both ears.

Example: *The old coot was deaf as a post, but he could sure play up a storm on his banjo!*

Dear John letter

Meaning: A note left by a lover saying the relationship is over.

Example: *Percy arrived home with a lovely bouquet of red roses on their third wedding anniversary, only to find a terse Dear John letter taped to the refrigerator door.*

Death before dishonor

Meaning: A soldier or activist attitude to never give up the fight or leave fallen comrades behind.

Example: *Corporal Reynolds ignored the threat, emerged from* *his position of cover and hustled out to retrieve the lifeless body of his fellow soldier, Private First-Class William T. Johnson, because Reynolds would gladly accept death before dishonor.*

Deep pockets

Meaning: A person or organization with a large amount of money backing them up.

Example: *The shady ambulance chaser took on the questionable personal injury case because he knew the insurance company would be on the hook and had very deep pockets.*

Deer in the headlights

Meaning: Stunned and temporarily immobile.

Example: *When Detectives walked attorney Yancy Quintana out the door in handcuffs, he had the distinctive deer in the headlights look plastered on his face.*

Deliver the goods

Meaning: Produce the desired results.

Example: *Tony "the Nose" wasn't being paid to do his "best efforts" in finding and dealing with the informant, he was being paid to deliver the goods.*

Devil's advocate

Meaning: Arguing the point of view of the opposition, to flush out its strengths and weaknesses.

Example: *Jimmy John suspected that forming a new label would not be in the music trio's best interests, and played the role of devil's advocate to test the downside of that idea.*

The devil's in the details

Meaning: The most difficult parts of any plan are hidden within the specifics.

Example: *Quincy hoped to help everyone thrive to their natural potential, but of course, the devil is in the details.*

Diamond in the rough

Meaning: Something or someone exquisite that simply needs some detail work to really shine up to full potential.

Example: *Young Simone didn't have all the moves and certainly wasn't a polished gymnast, but something about her told the Academy's owner she was a diamond in the rough.*

Diddly-squat

Meaning: Anything; nothing of any significance whatsoever.

Example: *What you think or say means diddly-squat to anybody here, so stand aside or get pushed aside.*

The die is cast

Meaning: The elements of a situation are so firmly set that the natural progression will be very predictable.

Example: *Once young Melissa Hickenlooper had tasted sweet success in shifter-cart racing, the die was cast and she went on to become the first woman to win the coveted F-1 Driver's Championship.*

Different kettle of fish

Meaning: Some activity with many significant differences beyond the other matter being considered

Example: *Writing a short poem one day at the beach was a simple and enjoyable task, but writing a play about the origins of Christianity—that was certainly a different kettle of fish.*

Different strokes for different folks

Meaning: Diversity in people results in diversity in likes and desires.

Example: *I can't say that I agree with my neighbor coddling her 7-year old son, but different strokes for different folks.*

Dig deep

Meaning: Use all your inspiration, effort, skill and focus.

Example: *The final words her coach gave her before she stepped up to the plate in the bottom of the ninth inning with the score tied, was to dig deep, and apparently that was all she needed for her to blast a walk-off homerun deep to right-centerfield.*

Dig your own grave

Meaning: Act in such a manner as to progressively and seriously worsen your situation.

Example: *The government spokesperson dug his own grave by repeatedly changing his advice, which was supposedly based on "science," and which ignored drastic consequences which were well-known to the general public.*

A dime a dozen

Meaning: Exceedingly inexpensive and readily available.

Example: *The two-bit prostitutes on the corner of Main Street* *and Broadway Avenue were a dime a dozen, but the lovely Melissa Quigley stood innocently on that corner, simply waiting for her taxi driver.*

A discerning eye

Meaning: A person with a well-developed ability to observe and analyze a particular situation.

Example: *The enchanting young woman had a discerning eye for fashion, having been mentored by her award-winning fashion design mother, Silvia Fabiano.*

Discretion is the better part of valor

Meaning: Sometimes the safest course is the most cautious, least confrontational, course.

Example: *Mixed martial artist, Ambrose Pennington, considered jumping into the drunken fray between the girl and her belligerent boyfriend, but since discretion is the better part of valor, she left it to the two of them to sort out their issues.*

Dish it out

Meaning: To dispense criticism to someone.

Example: *Cynthia was absolutely astute at dishing it out, but not so good at taking criticism about her arbitrary "boundaries" mantra.*

Dive into (something)

Meaning: To immerse oneself into a particular subject or activity.

Example: *Faced with insurmountable debt, Mortimer decided* *it was time to dive into the how-to books on filing Chapter 7, personal bankruptcy.*

Doctoring the ball

Meaning: A baseball term for surreptitiously attaching a foreign substance to a baseball to cause it to have erratic movement when pitched to a batter.

Example: *Ace hurler James "Jimbo" Jameson was unceremoniously ejected from the game when the savvy plate Umpire, Lucius Mendoza, caught Jimbo doctoring the ball.*

Dodge a/the bullet

Meaning: Narrowly avert disaster.

Example: *The six-man team attacking Mt. Everest ran out of oxygen in the Death Zone but dodged a bullet upon discovering a cache of unused oxygen bottles left behind by a previous team.*

Dog and pony show

Meaning: An orchestrated, over-dramatic display of actions and things intended to sell an idea or belief.

Example: *Captain Markowitz knew that Internal Affairs would put on a dog and pony show of inconclusive evidence and slanted witness testimony at his disciplinary hearing, but the Captain's ace in the hole was the testimony of his own key witness—the Chief of Police.*

The dog days of summer

Meaning: The hottest, most humid, days of summer, typically the 40 days from July 3rd to August 11 in the

Northern Hemisphere.

Example: *With the air conditioning on the fritz, it was umbrellas, fans and iced tea to keep us cool during the dog days of summer.*

Dog-eared

Meaning: Describing a small corner-section of a page, folded over to facilitate later access to it.

Example: *The first-year law student suddenly realized he had dog-eared almost every one of the 35-pages in his Torts casebook for the day's assignment on "proximate cause."*

Dog eat dog

Meaning: A tough, competitive environment where few favors are asked or granted.

Example: *When 15-yer-old Terrence Winterbottom stepped up to the table for the annual Texas State Fair Pie Eating Contest, he knew full well that it was dog eat dog from opening bell until the closing buzzer.*

Dog tired

Meaning: Exceptionally exhausted.

Example: *Surprisingly, he was dog tired after the five-mile Half Dome day hike, but he attributed the toll to his relative inactivity during the pandemic.*

Doing time

Meaning: Being incarcerated in a jail or prison.

Example: *The disgraced police officer had resigned himself to doing time for his ignominious crime spree.*

Do it by the book

Meaning: Accomplish something in strict accord with the rules, without illegal or otherwise prohibited shortcuts.

Example: *Officer Verthoffer was determined to do it by the book in execution of the search warrant, knowing that the prosecution case depended on the storage facility evidence.*

Dollars to donuts

Meaning: It is so very likely true.

Example: *That young kid is a fabulous athlete and dollars to donuts he's able to water ski the 31 miles from Long Beach to Avalon Bay with no problem.*

Doll face

Meaning: A term of endearment as a compliment for a beautiful woman.

Example: *Doll face, and so, you sit down while I teach this galoot a lesson he'll never forget.*

Do or die

Meaning: Give it every effort you've got, without regard to any potential adverse consequences.

Example: *With one loss in the round-robin stage of the Pan American badminton competition, it was do or die for the Men's Doubles pair from Mexico City.*

Don't beat around the bush

Meaning: Stop giving insignificant detail and get right to the point.

Example: *The impatient Jurist craned his head toward the freshman lawyer, Winifred Beasley, and barked, "Ms. Beasley, the jury is waiting to hear the meat of your closing remarks, so don't beat around the bush, and just get on with it!"*

Don't bite off more than you can chew

Meaning: Choose a task that is within your present capabilities, given all of the variables.

Example: *The gifted young artist wanted to try his hand at oil painting but was reluctant to bite off more than he could chew, selecting water color instead.*

Don't bite the hand that feeds you

Meaning: Show loyalty and respect to the person who supports or has helped you.

Example: *First Mate Bridger Cobblestecker elected to turn a blind eye to his Captain's occasional moral indiscretions, preferring to not bite the hand that feeds him.*

Don't burn your bridges (behind you)

Meaning: Retain as many viable options as possible from your past.

Example: *The Senator's intern was quietly warned not to burn her bridges if she wanted to have a future in the Democratic Party.*

Don't change horses in the middle of a stream
Meaning: Generally, don't change tactics or tools in the middle of an undertaking or job.
Example: *The Mexican Mafia decided to stick with Attorney Xavier Vinsar as counsel of record for their hitman, Jose Reynoso, preferring to not change horses in the middle of a stream.*

Don't/Do combine/mix business with pleasure
Meaning: It is generally best to keep work and personal activities separate and distinct.
Example: *If you mix business with pleasure, you stand the serious risk of accomplishing nothing useful in the process.*

Don't count your chickens before they're hatched
Meaning: Refrain from celebrating or planning based on a perceived victory prior to the activity actually concluding.
Example: *The Cuban ballplayer made the Rookie mistake of counting his chickens before they're hatched, and when applying for a U.S. Visa, he came to the rude awakening that his drug convictions would keep him out of the United States.*

Don't cry over spilled milk
Meaning: What's passed is past and should not affect your present attitude.
Example: *His dad dusted off his torn jeans, put the cowboy hat back on his head and told his son, "Bobbie, you can ride that horse, so don't cry over spilled milk."*

Don't cut off your nose to spite your face

Meaning: Once something negative has occurred, don't make it worse for yourself by some further misstep out of ego or frustration.

Example: *The fear was that the actor would cut off his nose to spite his face, but as he received his Best Actor Award, he thanked the casting community rather than accusing them of gross-incompetency and bias.*

Don't drop in on me, dude (Also, Don't take off on me, kook)

Meaning: A surfing term when a surfer deeper into the "peak" of a wave yells at another surfer out towards the "shoulder" of the wave, warning him or her not to paddle into ("take off on" or "drop in on") the wave and obstruct his ride.

Example: *At Waikiki Beach on Oahu, one of the local wolf-pack surfers yelled out, "Don't take off on me, kook," just as Californian Dexter Hooper paddled in exactly at the wave's peak.*

Don't give up your day job

Meaning: Contending that you're not good enough at an activity, such as being a violinist, to thrive financially without your normal, everyday, job.

Example: *The dispassionate bozo tossed the sidewalk-singer a One Dollar bill and crassly told him don't give up your day job.*

Don't go there

Meaning: Stop inquiring or commenting upon that line of thought.

Example: *Despite his innocent explanation, the enigmatic actress dismissed him with a disingenuous, "Please, don't even go there."*

Don't hold your breath
Meaning: What you're referring to is not going to happen, so there's no sense waiting in anticipation.
Example: *The man was putting up signs and told me he wanted Beverly Hills to change its zoning, to permit more high-density housing so that he and people like him could afford to live there, and I told him, "If that's what this is about, don't hold your breath."*

Don't let the fox guard the hen house
Meaning: Don't permit anyone with an adverse interest to protect information or resources which they are likely to exploit.
Example: *Following the robbery, Schmedly's Armored Car Service, Inc. learned to avoid hiring ex-felon bank robbers as Guards, finally understanding that you do not let the fox guard the hen house.*

Don't/Never play with fire
Meaning: Don't lightly ignore the high risk of harm from a dangerous activity.
Example: *Country Western icon, Jeffrey Q. Riverton, looked down at the pert young woman in the crowd and sang, "Never Play with Fire in my Heart."*

Don't pull your punches

    Meaning: Deal directly and comprehensively with a subject or activity.

    Example: *At the raucous Presidential rally, an onlooker yelled from about fifty yards back from the podium, "Don't pull your punches, Henry, just tell it like it is!"*

Don't/Never put all [of] your eggs in one basket

    Meaning: Diversify your resources so that a single setback does not take everything from you.

    Example: *When Grandpa Jones told the whippersnapper to never put all his eggs in one basket, little Leroy replied, "But I don't got no eggs, Grandpa, only this bow an' arrow set for thirteen ninety-five plus tax."*

Don't rock the boat

    Meaning: Go with the flow, in the sense of generally be a team player rather than causing problems.

    Example: *After the Sergeant cut the perp loose, he took the rookie cop aside and told him, "Don't rock the boat here, son, there's bigger forces in play than this two-time loser heroin addict."*

Don't shoot the messenger

    Meaning: Don't fault the person or entity communicating bad news if they are not the cause of the problem or difficulty.

    Example: *Fortunately for Pepe, the Baja Cartel knows that you* *don't shoot the messenger, at least not until you get your 2,000 kilos of yeyo back.*

Don't shoot yourself in the foot

Meaning: Be cautious to refrain from unnecessarily causing injury to your reputation, finances or physical self in any way.

Example: *Apparently the firearms instructor never heard the expression, "Don't shoot yourself in the foot," because—get this—he* literally *shot himself in the foot while demonstrating a quick-draw.*

Don't take any wooden nickels

Meaning: Often said in jest—a friendly warning to be careful in your everyday activities.

Example: *Heading off for my first year in college, Uncle Jim patted me on the back, waved goodbye and laughed as he hollered, "Don't take any wooden nickels!"*

Don't throw out the baby with the bath water

Meaning: Be careful not to lose, discard or destroy the larger or otherwise more important objective or thing when dealing with a lesser component of the situation.

Example: *The condescending Social Worker slowed her speech and explained that when you discipline your teenage child, it is always best to do it in a way where you do* not *throw out the baby with the bath water.*

Dot every "i" and cross every "t"

Meaning: Be methodically thorough and complete in detail.

Example: *The standard practice here is to dot every "i" and cross every "t," but in this particular case, we obviously did not rise to that gold standard.*

Do the trick

Meaning: Adequately satisfy the requirements of the particular task.

Example: *The eager young thespian decided that to get rid of the jitters, just before his audition he would cross his arms, tense up and vociferously state, "Get off me; get the hell offa me!" and that would do the trick.*

Do the dirty work

Meaning: Undertake the distasteful aspects of someone else's responsibilities.

Example: *The property manager was tasked with doing the owner's dirty work by posting notices to tenants of massive rent increases.*

Do's and don't's

Meaning: A concise list of acceptable and of unacceptable conduct.

Example: *When we arrived at Camp High Hill, we were each handed a list of do's and don't's, but as soon as we hit the pond, all of that went out the window.*

Double down

Meaning: Originally a gambling term, but now also—in some manner, to commit even more strongly to a position or action.

Example: *When the bank officer refused to open the vault, the robber doubled down by producing a firearm, pistol-whipping the man and threatening to shoot a teller if the safe were not opened within thirty seconds.*

A double-edged sword

Meaning: Something that could potentially be used both to give an advantage or benefits, and to give a disadvantage or detriment.

Example: *The particular clause of the premarital agreement was a tricky one as it could be used as a double-edged sword, but since the issue was whether a forfeiture would be upheld and because it is axiomatic that the law abhors a forfeiture, the clause was likely to be interpreted in a manner favorable to the wife.*

Double take

Meaning: Startled with an observation or in otherwise experiencing an event, or to revisit the memory to assure that you perceived it accurately.

Example: *Honestly, I did a double take when I saw you walking toward me, since I thought you'd been killed in Fallujah.*

Do you have it in black?

Meaning: A gay expression, meaning that the speaker prefers a black man's "equipment," so to speak.

Example: *He glanced up and stated to Harold, in a very matter-of-fact manner, "It's good, but do you have it in black?"*

Down and out

Meaning: Somewhat depressed or somber.

Example: *Not surprisingly, Attorney Ira Udderstoffen was a bit down and out after three Court Bailiffs dragged his client out of the room in shackles following a jury verdict of Guilty on seventeen Counts of Grand Larceny.*

Down, but not out

Meaning: Having suffered a setback but still actively pursuing the objective.

Example: *The Yukon Timberwolves' second-string goalie was down, but not out at the end of the Second Period, with a score of 3 to 2, Denver Racoons.*

Down for the count

Meaning: Having suffered a major setback from which he or she may not recover, or an overly dramatic exaggeration of a minor version of such.

Example: *The lovely Maleficent Miller was down for the count when her third Commercial Agent in six months dropped her, complaining, "You simply have got to shave your underarms!"*

Down in the doldrums

Meaning: With nothing good or positive happening; sad.

Example: *Captain Yardley was admittedly down in the doldrums upon watching his First Mate walk the plank, but he* *knew that for the ship to be safe and secure, even officers had to toe the line.*

Down the drain

Meaning: Irretrievably lost.

Example: *Once their Ace pitcher gave up 9 runs on 62 pitches in the top of the First Inning, the Marmot's chances of a Championship title were definitely down the drain.*

Down to brass tacks

Meaning: The essence of, or bottom line to, something.

Example: *Honey, let's get down to brass tacks—do you love me, or not?*

Down to earth

Meaning: Well-grounded in morality and culture; civil and approachable.

Example: *After all was said and done, if one did not know that he was a prolific serial killer, Jeff Mursetigan appeared to be a very down to earth guy.*

Down to the wire

Meaning: Nearing the end of allotted time for an activity.

Example: *It was right down to the wire when the exhausted lawyer descended on the Civil Clerk's Office to timely file his obligatory Notice of Appeal in the Piccadilly Square debacle.*

Drag (one's) heels

Meaning: Slow down the pace of one's work or decisions.

Example: *Stan had obviously been dragging his heels on disposing of his original, hard-shell foam Allen surfboard, and eventually he decided to keep it.*

Draw a line in the sand

Meaning: A decision that one will permit something so far and no further.

Example: *I drew a line in the sand, and when that snarling dog moved slightly closer to me, I sent it for a ride with a rear-leg, front thrust kick.*

Draw the line

Meaning: A decision that one will permit something so far and no further.

Example: *16-year-old Priscilla enjoys kissing but she draws the line at French kissing, explaining that, "It's yucky!"*

Drag (something) out

Meaning: Prolong some action unnecessarily, usually to accomplish some personal agenda.

Example: *Without a firm script to tie him down, the selfish actor was dragging the scene out for personal aggrandizement, and the foreign director just sat back and allowed him to do it.*

Dress (someone) down

Meaning: Chastise someone for failure to conduct oneself with decorum and competence.

Example: *When Tia received the umpire's Red Card for using* *profanity after her missed shot, her coach dressed her down with quiet intensity.*

Dress for the fall, not for the ride

Meaning: Prepare oneself to be capable of handling and withstanding failure, in the event that occurs.

Example: *We're in business to make money, but we dress for the fall, not for the ride, and we definitely don't cut corners on liability insurance.*

Dress to kill

Meaning: Dressing oneself in very alluring formal attire.

Example: *Tatiana needed to soften up the pharmaceutical executive in order to inveigle him into speaking freely about the drug trial protocols, so she dressed to kill for her dinner engagement.*

Dressed to the nines

Meaning: Dressing oneself in very attractive formal attire.

Example: *For closing argument, Bentley Simon Zeneker dressed to the nines to remind the jury he was one of the most powerful trial lawyers in the country.*

(To) drive a hard bargain

Meaning: Negotiate with strength and without major concessions.

Example: *Jackie drove a hard bargain and agreed to teach his childhood friend, Scott, the lyrics, melody and guitar chords to each new song for 25-cents per song.*

Drop a bombshell

Meaning: Suddenly reveal a highly inflammatory or momentous fact.

Example: *Coach Higgensipper walked to the press box and proceeded to drop a bombshell that their franchise quarterback was scheduled for transgender surgery after season's end.*

Drive (someone) up the wall

Meaning: Cause someone immense stress and grief.

Example: *With her overactive imagination and incessant questions, Shirley was driving her co-workers up the wall, but things calmed down when she began turning to the internet for answers.*

(To) drop a dime (on someone)

Meaning: To inform on a person or entity to law enforcement regarding suspected criminal wrongdoing.

Example: *Any poor soul stupid enough to drop a dime on another State Prison inmate would be put out of his misery within a week.*

Drop in the bucket

Meaning: A trifling; a very tiny part of a vastly larger whole.

Example: *The money spent on gas for the trip to San Diego was definitely an out-of-pocket expense, but it was a drop in the bucket compared to the attorney's fees to be earned on the seven-plaintiff personal injury lawsuit.*

Drop the ball

Meaning: To fail to discharge your responsibility to act in the furtherance of some activity or project.

Example: *As the two veteran writers parted company until the next session, Larry tossed Jack an errant tennis ball, commenting metaphorically, "Don't drop the ball."*

Drop the gloves

Meaning: To stop playing, competing or fighting easy and to get into it without holding back.

Example: *The squabbling neighbors each decided to drop the gloves and file competing Petitions for Injunctive relief.*

Drop the hammer

Meaning: Institute accountability and consequences.

Example: *Rufus had put up with a lot of grief from his space cadet employee, but he had to drop the hammer when she started showing up for work wearing various Nazi insignia.*

Dry as a bone

Meaning: Completely without appreciable moisture; exceptionally thirsty.

Example: *Having sat in the blazing sun for the better part of an hour, Oliver's wife-beater tee-shirt was dry as a bone by the time he covered up his undulating fat with another garment.*

Dry run

Meaning: A practice, or training, session for a particular activity or task.

Example: *To hone their speed and skills, a mock compound was constructed and the Rangers executed multiple dry runs of the compound's forced entry and the subject's rendition into American custody.*

Duck dive

Meaning: A surfing term for, scooting up to the "nose" of a surfboard, dipping forward underwater and allowing an oncoming wave to roll over the top of you.

Example: *Melissa Slim was caught inside and made the regrettable, albeit non-fatal, mistake of attempting to duck dive a ten-foot wall of whitewater.*

Ducks on the pond

Meaning: Mostly, but not exclusively, a baseball term, for a situation where two or three players are on base (baserunners) with a batter at the plate ready for his at-bat.

Example: *For as far as the eye could see, there were ducks on the pond throughout Bangkok, and the boys hardly knew which way to turn for hot Thai chicks.*

Dumb as a post

Meaning: Exceedingly limited in cognitive ability.

Example: *The carpenter's assistant was dumb as a post but he did come in handy in lifting heavy beams.*

To each, their own (or, Each to their own)

> **Meaning:** Each person has the right to his or her own personal preferences.
>
> **Example:** *Observing the octogenarian woman walking onto the beach wearing nothing but a flyaway hat and a bright orange, string bikini, Mattie laughed and remarked quietly to her sinuous girlfriend, "To each, their own."*

The early bird catches the worm

> **Meaning:** Often times, the person who starts working on a project the earliest, achieves an advantage in attaining his or her goals.
>
> **Example:** *Because the early bird catches the worm, the young shortboarder was eager to paddle out into the surf line at the crack of dawn, before the crowd arrived; but unfortunately for him, a marauding Great White Shark had the same idea.*

(Someone's) ears are burning

> **Meaning:** I am talking about someone on a sensitive subject.

Example: *Now that I described what she did with that guy, her ears are burning, for sure.*

Easy come, easy go

Meaning: Something acquired at little cost or effort, can also be lost the same way.

Example: *That summer, the girls seemed to flock to Hurley Harrison, but easy come, easy go and now they're not so interested for some reason.*

(Someone gets) egg on (their) face

Meaning: When a person is embarrassed from the course of events.

Example: *The company CEO had egg on his face after mistaking an employee's abdominal girth for a pregnancy, and when corrected by the young woman, he promptly apologized for the unfortunate congratulatory remarks.*

The elephant in the room

Meaning: The one, major obstacle or issue, recognition of which is being avoided for some reason.

Example: *Huddled within the Crisis Room of the White House, POTUS and his Cabinet Officers vigorously conversed on any number of marginally relevant subjects, but the elephant in the room was the bright, pink tricycle, with multi-colored handlebar streamers, which was parked neatly in a corner.*

Elvis has left the building

Meaning: Drawing on the analogy to Elvis Presley finally leaving a concert hall—an announcement tongue in cheek that the major personality of the event has departed from the venue.

Example: *Sustained applause could be heard following the announcement, "Well, folks, Elvis has left the building," causing V.P. of Marketing, Serenity Smithers, to smile slightly as she exited the convention hall doorway.*

The Emperor has no clothes on

Meaning: Spoken when people fail to acknowledge and affirm an obvious and unmistakable truth.

Example: *The smallish crowd apparently refused to acknowledge that the Emperor has no clothes on, and listened patiently to the politician's confusing and often garbled presentation.*

The end all, be all

Meaning: The ultimate, quintessential example or specimen of something.

Example: *Stephanie was the end all, be all of girlfriend prospects for me, since she was very pretty, slender, late-20s, a ski instructor, lived near me and loved badminton!*

End around

Meaning: Generally, but not exclusively, a football expression—a maneuver avoiding a direct confrontation with the primary obstacles, which nevertheless yields a strong chance of success.

Example: *The innovative criminal defense attorney had decided*

*to do an end around of the prosecution's case-in-chief
for auto-tampering, and called as his first witness a Sleep
Disorder specialist to testify that the defendant, Bob Perkins,
was unconscious due to somnambulism at the moment of the
alleged crime.*

Enough is enough

Meaning: What's been said or done should be adequate to settle the matter, once and for all.

Example: *A lead actor in the popular Soap Opera,* When the Earth Shakes, *stormed off the set, deciding that enough is enough when the director asked for the 17th take of his line, "Sure, easy for you."*

Etched in stone

Meaning: Established firmly and beyond change—usually stated in the negative.

Example: *The unspoken curfew was midnight, but it wasn't etched in stone and my parents were relieved to see me safe at home at twelve-fifteen.*

Even a broken clock is right twice a day

Meaning: A sarcastic comment that someone's accurate description of an event was blind luck and happenstance.

Example: *Denny Silverstone was quite proud of his "uncanny" prediction that the underdog player would beat the number-three seeded Chess Master, but his acquaintance Thomas P. Underhoven offered up that even a broken clock's right twice a day.*

Even keel

Meaning: A steady demeanor.

Example: *Attorney Silverstone was smart, but even more importantly, he had an even keel and wasn't affected by his adversary's inflammatory rhetoric.*

Every cloud has a silver lining

Meaning: When life deals out an unsavory and unwelcome outcome, there often is a highly desirable, hidden consequence.

Example: *As he was kicked to the curb by his ravishing, porn-star girlfriend, Gala Tyme, three-time loser and porn-actor-wannabe, Skip Beet, stumbled out the doorway, mumbling, "Every cloud has a silver lining."*

Every dog has his day

Meaning: Even an ordinary person without extraordinary skills sometimes will have an exceptional day's accomplishments.

Example: *The aging surfer was way over his head in this Semi-Final heat, but he also knew that every dog has his day, and paddled into a ten-foot face for a sick 9.8 ride.*

Every last one

Meaning: All of a particular category of things.

Example: *The robber didn't leave the bank until he had cleaned out every last one of the tellers' cash drawers, but his thorough work led to his arrest as the police were waiting when he walked out the door.*

Every mother's son

Meaning: Absolutely everyone.

Example: *I'm telling you, every mother's son was at that freedom protest marching over to City Hall.*

Everything but the kitchen sink

Meaning: Including everything you can think of and then some.

Example: *When Randolph P. Trimble, III returned to his Thailand condo following a six-month absence, he discovered that everything but the kitchen sink had been carted away by his now-ex-girlfriend—except for his acoustic, Martin D-28 guitar, which she had carefully placed on a small mat in the center of the Great Room.*

Everything under the sun

Meaning: Including everything you can think of and then some.

Example: *The 11-year old Freshman was so excited to get started with classes that he wanted to enroll in everything under the sun, but settled for 20-units of college credits that first Quarter at the University.*

An exception that proves the rule

Meaning: The minor exception to a rule that tends to prove the opposite, much more likely, result or explanation.

Example: *Bobby Rose, an immensely talented and skilled walk-on from a nothing-high school in Roanoke, Virginia, was an exception that proves the rule that top baseball college players originate from top baseball high school programs.*

Eye candy

Meaning: A physically attractive woman.

Example: *The soap opera leading man couldn't arrive at the Awards ceremony by himself, so he literally hired some eye candy to accompany him for the evening.*

Eye-opener

Meaning: Something that was particularly revealing about a situation.

Example: *Watching the City Councilman sell out to pharmaceutical-industry demands was a real eye-Opener and he turned up on the next hit-list for a recall campaign.*

(To) face the music

> **Meaning:** Openly accept the consequences for one's wrongful actions.
>
> **Example:** *With his State execution imminent and all appeals exhausted, it was finally time for the convicted serial killer, rap artist* Notorious Pop Sicle, *to face the music.*

A fact of life

> **Meaning:** Something that is a usual given for the vast majority of people.
>
> **Example:** *Occasional poverty was a fact of life for almost all professional actors, and yet they persevere.*

Fair and square

> **Meaning:** Free of undue advantage or deception.
>
> **Example:** *The Yorktown Alleycats overcame adversity and won the Championship softball game fair and square.*

Fair game
    Meaning: An acceptable target for criticism, acquisition or other exploitation.
    Example: *The outspoken actor was fair game for criticism, considering that he had earned $3,000,000 as an aging transgender female in* Naked and Afraid, *but publicly condemned any "marriage" except between a man and a woman.*

Fair to middlin'
    Meaning: Average to slightly above average.
    Example: *Asked how things were going, the 87-year-old paraplegic tipped his cowboy hat, adjusted his bolo tie and replied, "Fair to middlin', thanks, and yourself?".*

Fall off the turnip truck
    Meaning: Exhibiting signs of vast inexperience and foolishness—usually stated in the negative.
    Example: *I didn't just fall off the turnip truck and I won't fall for the old trick of looking for the penny in the bottom of a plastic bottle of water.*

Familiarity breeds contempt
    Meaning: Some personal background knowledge about someone often results in projection of ill-will and loss of respect.
    Example: *Kevin Canturbury learned first-hand that familiarity breeds contempt, when his kitty-corner neighbor wrote to the local* Rockingchair Gazette, *complaining about Kevin's, "exceedingly noisy, gas-guzzling Ferrari."*

Famous last words

>**Meaning:** Something which when stated, often times is a precursor for the exact opposite eventuality occurring.

>**Example:** *Your boat is too large to flounder in these six-foot seas?—Well, famous last words.*

Far and away

>**Meaning:** By far; substantially more.

>**Example:** *The digital artist was not the most articulate speaker at the Asians in Entertainment seminar, but the content of his comments was far and away the most thought-provoking.*

Far cry from

>**Meaning:** Not remotely comparable.

>**Example:** *For refined symmetry and unadulterated aesthetic beauty, the rather nondescript Shoebill of Eastern Africa is a far cry from the lovely and brilliantly colorful Rainbow Lorikeet of Australia.*

Faster than (one) can say Jack Robinson

>**Meaning:** Very quickly, in an exceptionally short period of time.

>**Example:** *When Buster Jenner spotted Matilda Smith at the school dance, faster than you can say Jack Robinson he asked her for a slow dance.*

Fat chance

>**Meaning:** Exceedingly unlikely.

>**Example:** *Outfielder Sonny Pitcairn knew that he had a fat*

chance of reaching the fly ball, but ran his heart out, took a mighty leap and surprised himself with a snow cone for the third out of the inning.

Fate worse than death

Meaning: An ignominious outcome to be avoided at all costs.

Example: *Losing a badminton match in two straight games to that marginally-skilled blowhard, Cornelius Cornpepper, was undeniably a fate worse than death, and I couldn't wait to extirpate the memory from my consciousness.*

Father time is undefeated

Meaning: Everyone eventually is adversely affected by the passage of time.

Example: *Unfortunately for sand volleyball enthusiasts throughout the world, father time is undefeated and Esther Minterwhoopen has finally announced her retirement at the conclusion of the present season.*

Fat of the land

Meaning: The finest and richest benefits.

Example: *The surly Nebraskan rancher, Ned Tully, had worked his tail off raising cattle on the Bar-T Ranch, and since reaching the age of 50, he's living off the fat of the land and enjoying every moment with his luscious Russian bride.*

Feast or famine

Meaning: That events of a certain type seem to either be exceedingly plentiful, or exceptionally rare.

Example: *A steady income was seemingly out of reach for Henry Botel, since the time-share condo industry tended to be feast or famine.*

Feather in (one's) cap

Meaning: Similar to a notch in one's gun handle—a symbol or prime example of one's accomplishments and skills.

Example: *Winning custody of the little girl to her father was a feather in my cap as a Family Law attorney, and it was particularly gratifying when the little girl thanked me and said, "You're a lawyer for kids."*

Feather (one's) own nest

Meaning: Adding to one's own self-interests or belongings in lieu of benefiting others in a more egalitarian manner.

Example: *There was a general consensus that to feather one's own nest with association funds was in poor taste, to say the least.*

Feel the pinch

Meaning: To experience the pressure of a difficult situation—particularly of a financial difficulty.

Example: *Red had a strong constitution when it came to fighting sickness and general adversity, but with the China Virus indirectly causing his roofing business to falter, he was definitely feeling the pinch.*

Feet on the ground

Meaning: Well-adjusted, practical, well-informed and

confident in one's demeanor, skills and ethics.

Example: *Mary Jean Siddecker was the perfect choice for President of the Mayfield P.T.A. since she had her feet on the ground plus five years of experience as Assistant to the Director of the Mayfield Cultural Center.*

(Something) fell/dropped like a lead balloon

Meaning: To precipitously and substantially fall due to gravity, or to decline rapidly in value.

Example: *When billionaire Mortimer Poppycock joked about the questionable value of the cryptocurrency Harvest Moon, its value fell like a lead balloon.*

Fence sitter

Meaning: Someone who declines to take sides on an issue.

Example: *Percy was an incorrigible fence sitter when it came to whether an mRNA Covid vaccine should or should not be mandated for children 12 and over in age.*

Fever pitch

Meaning: At a very high or rapid measure of effort.

Example: *In the last week prior to the gubernatorial recall election, campaigning for and against the sitting official was at a fever pitch.*

Few and far between

Meaning: Relatively rare.

Example: *The women in their 20s and 30s who were smart, appreciated older men, were not religious, were single and* *available, were attractive and athletic, were in shape and happened to cross my path were, to say the least, few and far between.*

A field day

Meaning: An opportunity for virtually unopposed success in the particular endeavor.

Example: *The My Lai soldiers had a field day killing vast numbers of innocent civilian villagers, but they would face Court-martial charges upon arriving back in the States.*

Fifteen minutes of fame

Meaning: Often expressed with a sarcastic intent—the very short-lived notoriety which seems to exist for every person, at least once in their lives.

Example: *The hit-and-run driver had his obligatory fifteen minutes of fame, as the cameras rolled while police cuffed him and hauled him away in a squad car.*

Fifth wheel

Meaning: An unnecessary and unwanted component to a group or mechanism.

Example: *The team manager and head coach both viewed Jim-Bob as a fifth wheel, but the players saw him as the alternative perspective needed in successful practices.*

Fight an uphill battle

Meaning: Struggling to overcome a difficult situation in which one is at a decisive disadvantage.

Example: *Melissa was fighting an uphill battle with the Human Resources Director, Eunice Merriweather, but after viewing several viral videos, Mrs. Merriweather finally saw the light and agreed that vaccinations would not be required at Acme Mechanical Supply, Inc..*

Fight fire with fire

Meaning: Meet the problem head-on with similar tactics used to create the problem in the first place.

Example: *The avowed atheist decided to fight fire with fire, by standing on a busy street corner in Huntington Beach, California and shouting, "Save yourself; do NOT believe in any god!"*

Fighting chance

Meaning: A reasonable opportunity for success.

Example: *The youngsters from Lowell Elementary School finally had a fighting chance in the Antelope Valley Junior Golf Classic, now that golf-guru David Heinen agreed to be their team's Golf Coach.*

Fight tooth and nail

Meaning: Give the effort of absolutely everything one has, without reservation.

Example: *The water ski racer phenom trailed the leader by 63 seconds rounding the Catalina mark, but on the leg home, he fought tooth and nail, soared into the lead and won the 52-mile race by 43 seconds for a new world record!*

Fill (someone's) boots

Meaning: Substantially match your qualities and abilities.

Example: *It was enormously unlikely that the back office could find anyone to fill Sorenson's boots as Left Forward for the Sunland Bladers, but they surprised us all when Rex Chin skated onto the ice for the game-day practice.*

Fine-feathered friend

Meaning: A humorous term of endearment—a compliment—for a friend, to indicate sophistication, attractiveness and even common interests.

Example: *Well, my fine-feathered friend, are you ready to get out on the town tonight and meet some gorgeous women?*

A fine kettle of fish

Meaning: A difficult and serious predicament.

Example: *The wifey had left me with a fine kettle of fish, having both my mother and mother-in-law stay over for the weekend—the same weekend.*

Fine print

Meaning: In law, the tedious detail of a contract which may well contain important and even unexpectedly draconian terms and conditions.

Example: *The impecunious coed was pleased to sign the house lease for the school year, but she might have been less excited had she bothered to read the onerous fine print.*

Fine-toothed comb

Meaning: With great and painstaking detail.

Example: *Detectives scoured the scene of the crime with a fine-toothed comb looking for that tell-tale drop of blood, and their efforts finally paid off when they spotted what appeared to be faint blood splatter on the foyer wall.*

Fire in the belly

Meaning: A strong passion for something, often leading to action.

Example: *If you don't have a fire in the belly for this sort of work, you should choose an avocation other than being a business litigation attorney.*

First things first

Meaning: Setting up a priority system where crucial matters are dealt with before other, related matters of lesser import.

Example: *Of course, it was first things first in "mitigating" external threats, after which we focused on helping the locals see us as caring individuals.*

Fish in a barrel

Meaning: Things to be performed, targeted or acquired which are readily visible, accessible and vulnerable.

Example: *In those days, attracting beautiful Thai women was literally like shooting fish in a barrel.*

Fish or cut bait

Meaning: Either do it now, or move on and forget about that objective.

Example: *The film producer knew that he had to fish or cut bait on his interest in Virgil Wannamaeker as the lead villain, and surprisingly, the producer chose to walk away.*

Fish out of water

Meaning: Someone who is in unfamiliar territory and not accustomed to operating in that environment.

Example: *The black youth from South Central Los Angeles was a fish out of water at Stanford University, but what he lacked in social skills, he more than made up for with his brilliant command of mathematics.*

A fishing expedition

Meaning: Actions which are intended more to expose hidden facts than to substantiate contentions based upon facts already known.

Example: *When the coppers hauled Mario Castellano out of the Caddie, the subsequent search was purely a fishing expedition that came up empty, resulting in Mario and his bodyguard/ driver being cut loose.*

Fit as a fiddle

Meaning: Describing a person—in quite good physical condition.

Example: *The old geezer was obviously fit as a fiddle, and with* *his lady, he danced circles around the younger men in their 60s and 70s.*

Fit to be tied

Meaning: So upset with a circumstance or event that it is almost overwhelming.

Example: *Professor Morningstar was fit to be tied upon discovering egregious plagiarism by Georgio Nostradamus, but she opted exposure in the student newspaper in lieu of expulsion.*

Five-finger discount

Meaning: Stealing something.

Example: *It's not that stealing was particularly gratifying to the young ne'er-do-well, but simply that the five-finger discount saved a lotta cash otherwise spent on bling.*

Fixin' to (do it)

Meaning: A primarily Southern expression—getting ready to, eventually, undertake some particular activity.

Example: *In a deep Southern drawl, the youngster carefully replied, "Well sure ma, I been fixin' to paint that fence real quick now, sometime soon, when I can."*

Flat out

Meaning: The fastest speed of which one is capable.

Example: *I gassed it, hoping that if I were flat out I could make it without hitting the far side of the ditch and bending my forks, not to mention my body.*

(To) flatten a nickel

Meaning: To be incarcerated on a sentence of five years in State Prison.

Example: *For the Sullivan family, it was a double tragedy as Michael Sullivan was sentenced to flatten a nickel in the California State Prison system for the negligent homicide of his own young son, Brad.*

Flesh and blood

Meaning: Family linked by close genetic relations.

Example: *She was my own flesh and blood, and so yes, I did take her murder very personally.*

Flip-flop

Meaning: Vacillate from one decision or point-of-view on a subject to an opposing position on the subject.

Example: *The CEO has flip-flopped multiple times now on this issue and it's creating some real hardship among certain employees trying to understand their future as Valets for the Racetrack.*

Flip-flops

Meaning: Sandals with no heal strap and a strap originating between the big toe and the next toe.

Example: *Tank tops and flip-flops seemed to qualify as "shirts and shoes" for this quaint beachside café.*

Flip the script

Meaning: Alter the *expected* outcome to the opposite result, especially in a contest or competition.

Example: *With a pick-six in the first Quarter, and the Badgers' fumble leading to another touchdown in the closing seconds of the first half, the Ducks have flipped the script, with a 14 – 0 lead over the Badgers heading into the second half.*

Flying high

Meaning: Elated at one's success.

Example: *Eunice was flying high on the news that her credit had been approved for a loan to purchase the new sports car convertible.*

Fly in the face of

Meaning: Contradicts.

Example: *Religious prayer, in public schools, flies in the face of the doctrine of Separation of Church and State, and cannot be permitted.*

Fly in the ointment

Meaning: The thing that keeps something else from being perfectly designed or planned.

Example: *The fact that Wednesdays happened to be the day when the bank vault had the least money on hand, was certainly a fly in the ointment upon which the lead bank robber had not planned.*

Fly off the handle

Meaning: Explode in anger or frustration.

Example: *It wasn't every day that Chief Lifeguard, Amos Yearling, would fly off the handle, but hearing that a Jeep driven by Lifeguard Pearlman had actually run over a guest sleeping on the sand, was enough to trigger his latest tirade.*

Fly off the shelves

Meaning: Selling very rapidly.

Example: *The pandemic caused toilet paper to fly off the shelves, but many people couldn't be bothered searching for the truth about the origins of the Covid virus.*

Fly the coup

Meaning: To escape from somewhere.

Example: *The insolent young boy was ordered to remain in school detention for the remainder of the afternoon, but he flew the coup and was last seen headed to the river with his fishing pole.*

Folded up like a cheap suit

Meaning: Succumbing to pressure, making a series of costly mistakes.

Example: *Golf Pro Evander Cloninger was in close contention for the lead, but folded up like a cheap suit on the final three holes.*

A fool and his money are soon parted

Meaning: When a careless person somehow comes into a lot of money, it won't last long.

Example: *It was no surprise that the Seven Million in lottery winnings lasted less than a year, since a fool and his money are soon parted.*

A fool's errand

Meaning: An activity doomed to failure from the start with very little upside.

Example: *It was a fool's errand to ask the devoted thespian if she wanted to quit the acting profession.*

Foot the bill

Meaning: When you pay for something that benefits others as well as you.

Example: *It was his daughter's 17th birthday, so of course her somewhat obsequious father agreed to foot the bill for Melissa and ten of her closest friends to go to the amusement park.*

For my money

Meaning: In my judgment or opinion.

Example: *Julie has a cute smile and Sapphire has a nice booty, but for my money, Priscilla's sense of humor makes her the most attractive of the three.*

For the birds

Meaning: Not a good choice.

Example: *With all the rain, wind and choppy waves, this surf trip's been for the birds and I say let's make it home.*

Foregone conclusion

> **Meaning:** Something that has already, in effect, been determined by prior events.
>
> **Example:** *Half-way through the date with Emily Pinevale, it was a foregone conclusion she wouldn't make out with me, and then she proved me so wrong.*

For the time being

> **Meaning:** Presently, until some intervening factor or revelation comes into play.
>
> **Example:** *Mindy was willing to defer her first kiss with Stanley for the time being, but he wasn't getting off that easily and she held his hand during their very first romantic walk in the park.*

(To be) fresh as a daisy

> **Meaning:** A humorous expression—describing a person who is clean, well-rested and alert.
>
> **Example:** *The drunken cow poke sat up in the water trough, spit out some filthy water and exclaimed, "Yes sir, I am as sober as a mouse church—er, as fresh as a daisy!"*

Freudian slip

> **Meaning:** A subconscious process where one's true beliefs are inadvertently revealed through something intentionally stated.
>
> **Example:** *In quite a Freudian slip, as they were leaving for their date, Terrence told Mable, "You look beautiful tonight, particularly your undress, I mean, dress, your dress."*

Friendly fire

Meaning: Projectiles or explosives coming from one's own forces or allies, particularly fire that may result in injury or death to the same side.

Example: *The gunny and his platoon were between a rock and a hard place as the enemy was attacking from the south and friendly fire was cascading in from the north.*

(To have) a frog in (one's) throat

Meaning: Where one's throat is slightly obstructed, causing the voice to sound coarse and uneven.

Example: *Despite the usual, tedious warm-up routines, famed Oli Ristorini, baritone, faltered in his opening bars as Figaro in* The Marriage of Figaro, *thanks to a frog in his throat.*

From scratch

Meaning: Starting with only the basic raw materials.

Example: *As kids, we put together the first skateboards from scratch, with only metal roller skates and two-by-fours to work with.*

From the bottom of my heart

Meaning: With the deepest possible emotion and gratitude.

Example: *At my father's funeral, I wished him farewell, and from the bottom of my heart I said that I will miss him.*

From the get-go

Meaning: Starting at or applying to the entire process or event, from the very beginning to its conclusion.

Example: *We knew from the get-go these thugs wanted our money, and we weren't about to accommodate them in any manner whatsoever.*

From the word "go"

Meaning: At the extreme outset of an action, activity or event.

Example: *Jack was infatuated with the lithe Asian woman from the word "go," and plotted to insinuate himself into her life through their mutual interest of badminton.*

From your lips to god's ears

Meaning: Hoping that what you have just said comes to actual fruition.

Example: *Thrilled with his notion that she'd be cast as the title character in* Norma, *soprano Edna Drovenosky whispered, "From your lips to god's ears."*

From rags to riches

Meaning: From humble beginnings to incredible financial or social success.

Example: *It was not the classic tale of from rags to riches—considering that his mother had gifted him $100,000 in cash upon graduation from law school—but it was close enough for this self-made billionaire.*

From whole cloth

Meaning: Starting from nothing and building upon that.

Example: *The devious con-artist spun his exonerating lies from whole cloth and the detectives bought the colorful story, hook, line and sinker.*

Front page news

Meaning: Very important and timely information.

Example: *If it were front page news, I could understand my mother running out of the house at the last minute to catch me before I drove away, but bless her heart, she just wanted to give me another kiss goodbye for my drive up to Santa Barbara.*

Full circle

Meaning: From the beginnings to the outer reaches and around again to the beginnings.

Example: *When I spotted Joanne standing there, I realized that both of us had lived our lives full circle, but that those circles had simply not overlapped.*

Full-court press

Meaning: Originally a basketball term—full opposition, involving all team members, from the beginning of the opposition's efforts until the opposition is defeated.

Example: *Yes, and I know, they're way ahead in annual sales, but we're going to take the lead, as a team, with a full-court press!*

The full monty

Meaning: Whatever is referred to is clearly the most outlandish, creative and complete.

Example: *April and Eunice decided to go the full monty in their* *lemonade stand enterprise, decorating the table in bright-colored flowers and lemon peels, and wearing yellow, spring dresses, with pink and yellow ribbons on their wrists.*

(To be) full of beans

Meaning: In particular, as used within the United States—to be untruthful and nonsensical.

Example: *It had never happened and the young boy was simply full of beans—at least according to the wrinkled and rickety old man.*

Full speed/steam ahead [or] Full throttle

Meaning: Move forward without delay, on unrestrained power, without holding back.

Example: *The Scoutmaster turned to his hesitant, albeit attentive, troop of boys and confided with them, "I know they're bigger and older, but Troop 295 can win this soccer match, if you all do your best and go full steam ahead!"*

G

A game of cat and mouse

Meaning: A process of pursuit, near-catches and evasion, repeated over and over.

Example: *The indefatigable Detective was engaged in a deadly game of cat and mouse with the illusive serial killer, who at each crucial step, seemed to have an uncanny knack of escaping the net.*

Game on

Meaning: The challenge and opposition have commenced.

Example: *I had thought I was in love, and maybe I had been, but when she excluded me from a party with her friends, it was game on and I wanted a divorce.*

Game plan

Meaning: A strategy worked out in advance for some activity.

Example: *They had the basic idea, now all they needed was to work up the game plan for impeaching the Governor for immoral and dishonest conduct in office.*

Garden variety

Meaning: A common form of something, qualitatively indistinguishable from other such common forms.

Example: *The first guitar that the boy possessed was a garden variety, steel-string acoustic, but by the time he turned 16, James owned the finest steel-string Reynoso acoustic guitar that money could buy.*

A gentleman and a scholar

Meaning: A complimentary reference to a male indicating that he is a reasonable and intelligent man of good moral character.

Example: *The illustrious philanthropist, Christopher Hutchinson, was not only a gentleman and a scholar, but he was a Master wood carver to boot.*

Get a grip

Meaning: Calm down and think rationally.

Example: *The screaming Karen needed to get a grip and accept the fact that the attractive young woman parking in the Handicap parking space had the absolute right to be there, particularly considering that she was a double-amputee.*

Get (someone) a leg up

Meaning: Assist someone who is at a disadvantage and needs help.

Example: *My dad had his faults for sure, but one piece of advice I always respected was to get someone a leg up if the cards were stacked against them.*

Get a second wind

Meaning: To recover enough from a recent difficult effort, such that one is again ready to compete or fight.

Example: *Number 4, Rockodile Dundee, seemed to get a second wind after three furlongs, and charged up from the rear to place a respectable second in the famed Willow Dale Derby.*

Get a taste of your/their own medicine

Meaning: Suffer through hardship or pain similar to that which one earlier dealt out to another.

Example: *Ron Gronkowsky got a taste of his own medicine when his girlfriend lied about her plans and enjoyed a weekend getaway with his best friend, Jim Smithers.*

(To) get away with murder

Meaning: To escape justice for an egregious wrong.

Example: *An unscrupulous businesswoman from the word "go," Anne Ventura seemed to get away with murder in her latest nefarious scheme, only to be foiled by the inimitable Detective Sam Slater.*

(To) get (someone's) goat

Meaning: To infuriate someone by attacking them where it hurts the most, emotionally.

Example: *The lovely yet playfully vindictive Melissa Farmington was determined to get her boyfriend's goat by dancing with his brother at the Harlan County Fair.*

Get into deep water

Meaning: Get into very serious trouble in some immediate dealing.

Example: *The desperate lawyer got into deep water when she offered to write a Last Will and Testament for the couple, despite the fact that she was by trade, a criminal defense attorney.*

Get lost

Meaning: A crude directive by someone to someone else to leave somewhere immediately.

Example: *These bozos were bothering my old lady, so I warned 'em to get lost, and when they didn't, I put their lights out.*

(To) get/have my/your ducks in a row

Meaning: To adequately prepare, with a strategy and adequate recourses, for a present or imminent difficulty.

Example: *Stephanie wanted to have all her ducks in a row before confronting her step-mother about mismanagement of the family trust assets.*

(To) get off on the wrong foot

Meaning: To begin a relationship or encounter with another poorly, in an unintended adverse manner.

Example: *The best-of-intentions, albeit highly stressed housewife, apologized to her lawyer for getting off on the wrong foot in their attorney-client relationship, and promised to pay the overdue retainer sum the following week.*

(To) get on/off your high horse

Meaning: Accusing one of being condescending or sanctimonious.

Example: *Please, get off your high horse, Mister Chesbrough, before I call an emergency Board of Directors meeting and have you replaced as CEO!*

(To) get on (one's) nerves

Meaning: To do something repeatedly that annoys someone else to distraction.

Example: *In Sixth Grade, Darlene Peacock was by far the best kickball player on the playground, but her natural athleticism did get on some of the other, less-athletic, girls' nerves.*

(To) get on/off your soapbox

Meaning: To lecture others on some controversial subject; or to be directed to refrain from doing that.

Example: *Nonplused with the speaker's remarks, the crowd was more or less quiet and courteous, at least until someone in the back yelled out, "Get off your soap box, Dr. Finkel!"*

(To) get out of Dodge

Meaning: To actually and physically depart from some place (as opposed to *preparing* to depart), especially from a town or city.

Example: *The drive to San Diego would only take about an hour and a half, but getting out of Dodge, for reasons only my wife could explain, took an inordinate amount of time.*

Get over it

> **Meaning:** Move on and stop dwelling on something in particular, in the past.
>
> **Example:** *As a thespian auditioning, if you can't get over it, try a different profession.*

Get real

> **Meaning:** Be reasonable, realistic and serious.
>
> **Example:** *When his buddy dared him to paddle out on the triple-overhead day in Huntington Beach, California, Murphy stared at the monstrous waves and replied, "Get real, Tony."*

Get (someone) the axe

> **Meaning:** To terminate the employment of someone.
>
> **Example:** *They wanted to lower their payroll without running afoul of age-discrimination prohibitions, so the Board of Directors voted to simply give* everyone *the axe who refused to get vaccinated, and when the smoke cleared, 40% of those people were over 50 years old!*

Get the ball rolling

> **Meaning:** To get things started with some gesture or action.
>
> **Example:** *Young Gertrude Finnigan decided to get the ball rolling by sitting right next to Johnny Baker at lunch time.*

Get the lead out

> **Meaning:** Stop slacking and put more effort and energy into the activity.

Example: *The Sergeant barked out his orders to the new recruits to get the lead out, and if by some sad twist of fate, they ignored him, they would pay for it with sit-ups and push-ups for hours.*

Get the picture

Meaning: Understand an overview of the situation.

Example: *If Veronica Honeywell didn't get the picture by now, she wouldn't have long to wait, considering that the sexually harassing Vice President was headed into her office as we speak.*

Getting out of hand

Meaning: Becoming unmanageable, disruptive, dangerous or chaotic.

Example: *The school district's disciplinary process was getting out of hand, to say the least, when they threatened suspensions without pay for employee conduct which clearly amounted to constitutionally protected freedom of religion acts.*

Get up and go

Meaning: Vim, vigor, energy and a positive attitude.

Example: *I've always had enough get up and go for ten men, but when I've had a big day, I'm down for the count physically and mentally and just need to relax.*

(To) get up and down

Meaning: A golfing term—to hit a golf ball onto the green at a stroke count *greater* than two strokes prior to par, and to "hole" the ball in only one put.

Example: *On the 17th hole known as The Terminator, Oliver Trigginhoffer was laying 3 on the fairway, but he still hoped to get up and down for a par five.*

(To) get up on the wrong side of the bed

Meaning: To wake up in a bad mood at the start of the day.

Example: *Obviously, he got up on the wrong side of the bed and Cynthia decided to extricate herself from the premises by taking a morning run.*

Get with the flow

Meaning: To join in to the general direction, mood and strategies of the team or working-group as a whole.

Example: *Bill Bleeker entreated the young executive to get with the flow by the next Monday morning employee meeting.*

(To) get you coming and going

Meaning: They take something from you, regardless of the way you turn or divert.

Example: *Between sales tax on everything you buy, to income tax on everything you make, the tax man gets you coming and going until nothing is left for necessities.*

Get your feet wet

Meaning: Try something out for the first time to get some experience in the activity.

Example: *The waitress had never played badminton before, so I told her to meet me over at the badminton club, get her feet wet and she'll like it.*

Give and take

> **Meaning:** An attitude or situation where compromise is feasible, involving some manner of *quid pro quo*, where each side receives something of value.
>
> **Example:** *In a healthy relationship between Actor and Director, there should be give and take—but not all such relationships are healthy.*

Give (someone) a run for their money

> **Meaning:** Engage in the contest, game, business or other competition in such a manner that it is not completely one-sided for the opposition and where there is a reasonable chance to prevail.
>
> **Example:** *Despite the age-issue, the capable thespian was determined to give her competition a run for their money at the screen test, and the rest is history.*

Give (someone) a wide berth

> **Meaning:** Allow and give ample space, physically or psychologically.
>
> **Example:** *After consuming an excessive volume of tequila the evening before, the slightly-sloshed government attorney was careful to give all co-workers and Court personnel a wide berth until the alcohol was completely out of his system.*

Give him an inch and he'll take a mile

> **Meaning:** Where once you make any small concession, the opposition, or person or thing under your direction, will

use that as justification for taking and demanding more and more.

Example: *His trainer had to be particularly careful in implementing correct and consistent natural and artificial riding aids, for Iceman was a very clever horse and if you gave him an inch, he'd take a mile in deviating from any plan but his own.*

Give him enough rope, he'll hang himself

Meaning: Where the opposition, given the opportunity and latitude, will defeat him or herself without your further assistance.

Example: *Following the inconclusive interrogation efforts, Captain Sanchez elected to release the cat-burglar suspect, and have a team of undercover officers shadow him 24/7, on the theory that if you give a man enough rope, he'll hang himself.*

Give it your/my best shot

Meaning: Put one's best effort in toward success.

Example: *The pint-sized T-baller decided to give it her best shot, stepped up to the plate, and blasted the ball, yard, over the left-field fence!*

Give me a break

Meaning: Stated sarcastically—stop lying, exaggerating or embellishing to me.

Example: *When the dogmatic coed regurgitated her absurd supposition that the earth was flat, her Physics Major friend simply replied, "Marley, please, just give me a break," and smiled.*

Give (one's) eye teeth

Meaning: On a personal basis, it has great value to me.

Example: *Baseball is such a big part of my life, I would give my eye teeth to have a baseball glove from the early days.*

Give/get (someone) the boot

Meaning: To terminate someone from employment, a relationship or a place.

Example: *This guy got so drunk, he was touching waitresses and picking fights, so we had to give him the boot—we 86'd him right to the street—and that was that.*

Give the high sign

Meaning: Physically signal to another person, in some obvious or pre-determined manner, that the plan, whatever it is, is on and ready to execute, and that the "game is afoot," as Sherlock Holmes would say.

Example: *When you give the high sign, I'll walk up to you two as if it were a chance meeting and you can introduce me.*

Give the shirt off (one's) back

Meaning: To be very generous, putting the recipient's interests before one's own.

Example: *Iris Winterlochen would gladly give the shirt off her back to help her loving grandmother, who was always there for her when she was growing up.*

Give up the ghost

Meaning: Recognizing that it is a lost cause, to stop trying to do something.

Example: *Dale Andert wanted to meet up for lunch and a few brewskies at his local watering hole, Pelican's Roost, but decided to give up the ghost when his friends insisted on a quaint restaurant in Belmont Shore known as Shore Thing.*

Glass ceiling

Meaning: A hidden but very real barrier that stands against certain categories of people from advancing in their field of employment.

Example: *Willie Johnson was excited to have been hired into a prestigious Boston law firm, but after one year as a lawyer, he realized that a glass ceiling against blacks was blocking him from moving above summarizing deposition transcripts.*

Glimmer of hope

Meaning: Something that signals a change for the better.

Example: *Willie felt a glimmer of hope when, after authoring a juvenile law, law review, article titled* A Dangerous Commitment, *the doors to success in that Boston law firm were finally opening for him.*

Go against the grain

Meaning: Taking the difficult path with the most resistance in a manner or direction which one would not ordinarily undertake.

Example: *Shortstop Ty Upton was going against the grain* *when he insisted on focusing on the basics, at the beginning of his minor league baseball career.*

Go ahead, make my day

Meaning: Popularized by Clint Eastwood as Harry Callahan in the feature film, *Dirty Harry*—in effect, daring someone to make a move, the consequences of which will be tragic for the one accepting the dare and a personal coup for the person making the dare.

Example: *Challenging his dog Simone to get past him on the front lawn, Willard remarked, "Go ahead, make my day," whereupon Simone zipped effortlessly past him, avoiding the tag.*

Go all in

Meaning: Especially a no-limit poker term, but also used elsewhere—to make a full commitment of all resources as your wager or stake in the outcome, requiring a meeting of that bet or a corresponding all-in by one's opponent if they cannot meet the wager dollar-for-dollar.

Example: *The normally cautious day-trader had such a strong feeling about the market trend that on Monday night at 11:32 p.m. he went all-in on the Bread Basket cryptocurrency, and by morning, his investment had risen by over 120%, a gain of some $420,000 in the span of eight wonderful hours.*

Go bananas

Meaning: To react in a bizarre, crazy or incredibly emotional and unrestrained manner.

Example: *The plan was for Mister White to throw his drink*

*on Miss Green and for her to go bananas creating the requisite
distraction, while Mister Blue emptied the till of the restaurant's
daily take.*

Go belly up

Meaning: To comprehensively fail financially or otherwise,
usually in a business activity.

Example: *Whether a corner lemonade stand could go belly up
from mismanagement was no longer a matter of idle speculation,
since the cups and sugar alone cost more than the 5-cent drink
price set by the youthful entrepreneurs, Benjamin and Gavin
Bettlechin.*

Go cold turkey

Meaning: Ceasing some habitual activity without any drugs
or other, outside assistance.

Example: *Now under arrest and charged with 17 Counts of
Armed Robbery, Miguel Martinez was forced to go cold turkey in
overcoming his insidious heroin addiction.*

Goes sideways

Meaning: The process of an activity falling off from
operating smoothly and successfully.

Example: *The game went sideways when Vinnie air-mailed his
throw thirty feet over the third baseman's glove and the go-ahead
run scored.*

Go down swinging

Meaning: If one is going to fail, it will be a failure while fighting for success.

Example: *Mister Hilliard might get fired for speaking up for prayer in school, but he was dead set to go down swinging.*

(To) go down in flames

Meaning: Originally a war time expression in aeronautics—to lose a battle, contest or other activity in a spectacular display of defeat.

Example: *Orelius Mohammed Jabar was a brilliant Grandmaster from Queens, but in the U.S. Open Chess Championships he went down in flames in straight games to a 13-year old prodigy, Petunia Pinelli of Huntington Beach.*

(To) go down with the ship

Meaning: For one to stick with the ill-fated project to the very end.

Example: *As the Lancaster Knitting Bee started to unravel—no pun intended—with fewer participating knitters every week, its founder, the lovely and amiable Emily Perkins, announced that she intended to go down with the ship, and encouraged other stalwart knitters to do the same!*

(To) go Dutch

Meaning: As between two or more persons meeting up during an activity which will cost money, for each person to pay their own share of the expense.

Example: *Jamal Jones asked Julie Rickenbacker if she wouldn't mind going Dutch on their first date, and Julie eagerly consented as they mapped out their upcoming Miniature Golf escapade.*

God's green earth

    Meaning: An expression of surprise or astonishment, similar to "what in the world?...", meaning "how?" or "what?".

    Example: *How in God's green earth do you expect to get those permanent marker scribbles off of your face, Jimmy?*

(It) goes south

    Meaning: When things take a decisive turn for the worse.

    Example: *After the contumacious youngster kicked dirt on the Home Plate Umpire's shoes, things went south very quickly, culminating with the Umpire ejecting the boy not only from the game, but from the entire Sports Complex!*

Goes/going yard

    Meaning: A baseball expression—hitting a Home Run where the batter literally hits the pitched baseball in fair territory out of the playing field.

    Example: *With two outs in the top of the Ninth, Teddy Witherspoon of the San Jose Gophers hammered an inside fastball, deep to left-center field, going yard for the go-ahead run over the Bakersfield Rounders.*

Go fly a kite

    Meaning: Get away, forget about it, it's not going to happen.

    Example: *I'll never forget the night—I was about 14 at the time—my dad stood up to a huge college dude at a drive-in movie* *who was trying to "save" a spot, and he told that guy, "Go fly a kite, we're parking here"!*

Go for broke

Meaning: Put every effort and resource into the pursuit.

Example: *Barney Huddleston exclaimed, "This year, I'm goin' for broke!", moments before losing to his Aunt Gertrude in the Huddleston Memorial Horseshoes competition.*

Go hand-in-hand

Meaning: The various things operate in conjunction with each other.

Example: *Modesty often goes hand-in-hand with integrity.*

Go hog wild

Meaning: Act with extreme and unrestrained excitement.

Example: *When the Buffalo Bobcats won their first-ever New York Water Polo Championship, the high school team went hog wild, tossing their coach into the pool in celebration.*

Going/headed on a wild goose chase

Meaning: Search for something which either does not exist or which does not exist anywhere close to where you are searching.

Example: *Although the Sheriff suspected they were headed on a wild goose chase, she and her team of Deputies and volunteers alike proceeded to search the forested area, which had been divided into one-mile-square grids.*

Going the extra mile
> **Meaning:** Make a substantial effort, well beyond what could reasonably be expected.
> **Example:** *The affable tug boat Captain, Piers Pulliam, would always go the extra mile for his crew, pitching in whenever possible for even the most mundane of chores.*

Golden opportunity
> **Meaning:** Circumstances which greatly favor one's success in an important endeavor.
> **Example:** *The film audition for the role of a swim instructor, fighting to the death in a lap pool, was a golden opportunity for actor Stan Parker, who had played water polo in high school, was an ocean beach lifeguard for years during college and was a proficient Black Belt in Kenpo Karate.*

The gold standard
> **Meaning:** The highest iteration of quality for a category of goods and services.
> **Example:** *The executive jet leasing service offered the gold standard and did not disappoint in any department.*

Good as gold
> **Meaning:** Something that has been proven to exist to a virtual certainty; completely genuine.
> **Example:** *Our inside man at the tire factory tells us worker support for unionizing is as good as gold and that we should move on that post-haste.*

Good riddance to bad rubbish

Meaning: Happy to see something or someone leave or be sent away from one's presence.

Example: *There was a unanimous sentiment of good riddance to bad rubbish when the dishonored CEO was escorted by Security out the front door, carrying only a cardboard box of personal items.*

Good to go

Meaning: Ready to proceed.

Example: *Once she had all her safety gear on, she was good to go on her Honda 500 XR for the 180-mile trek across the Baja Peninsula, through Mike's Sky Ranch and into San Felipe, Mexico.*

A goose-egg

Meaning: Empty; zero.

Example: *The reading was top drawer, but ultimately, I came up with a goose-egg.*

Go overboard

Meaning: Act in a manner which is excessive under all of the circumstances.

Example: *Dino knew that he went a little bit overboard on the barbecue cuisine, but he wanted to make a favorable impression on his new friends, and hope that they never suspected he was in Witness Protection.*

Go over like a lead balloon

Meaning: ("lead" as in the metal) The referred to proposed action will not be favorably considered.

Example: *Full-face masks and violence as the means of persuasion at the rally will go over like a lead balloon.*

(Someone's) got a bone to pick with (someone)

Meaning: Someone has a complaint to or dispute with someone else.

Example: *One day, my father showed me a spot on his favorite tie that I had borrowed the night before, and he said, "I've got a bone to pick with you, son."*

Go the distance

Meaning: Originally a boxing term—Sticking with a fight or other difficult effort to the very end.

Example: *The stunning Beatrice Cumberbatch was uncertain if she could go the distance with Acme Adult Motion Pictures, but she decided to approach the job one film at a time.*

Go to bat for (someone)

Meaning: To actively support someone in their conduct or proposed actions.

Example: *Victor Martinez gladly went to bat for his 10-year-old son, Julio, when Julio was suspended for wearing an American Flag pin on his jacket at school.*

Go-to guy

Meaning: The contact-person of choice in a particular area of activity.

Example: *Benito Chavez was the go-to guy for negotiating and drafting rock-solid Premarital Agreements.*

Go under the knife

Meaning: Undergo a surgical procedure.

Example: *To placate her officious Manager, the aging superstar reluctantly agreed to go under the knife, again—this time to raise her sagging upper eyelids.*

Grain of salt

Meaning: Healthy skepticism in the face of somewhat dubious claims.

Example: *My 9-year-old son was taught in school that he should personally feel guilty for slavery in America which occurred hundreds of years ago, and I simply mentioned, he should take that kind of instruction with a grain of salt.*

Grandfather clause [or,] Grandfathered in

Meaning: A provision that makes exceptions, to a general policy, for people or things in existence for a certain number of years prior to institution of the policy.

Example: *Fortunately, there was a grandfather clause allowing monthly rentals for condominiums owned prior to the new policy going into effect; so, my condo was grandfathered in.*

Grass roots

Meaning: A decentralized conglomeration of basic supporters.

Example: *There was a nationally-widespread, grass roots support for the right to bear arms in the United States of America.*

Graveyard shift

Meaning: A job where the shift-hours are approximately from midnight until 8:00 a.m..

Example: *I politely reminded my dad that during the summer following my college Freshman year, my job at the tire factory had been swing shift, not graveyard shift.*

Gravy train

Meaning: Some particular source of income or profit that is unusually lucrative and ongoing.

Example: *The financial advisor knew a gravy train when he saw one, and was quick to invite billionaire Mikael Rickenbacker to a business planning seminar.*

Grease the skids

Meaning: To give something, such as a payoff, sexual services or some other form of benefit, to someone intended as a *quid pro quo* for favorable consideration on some topic or activity.

Example: *With the Opera House remediation project on the line, Big Tony was assigned the delicate task of meeting with Councilman Stevens to grease the skids for the American Brotherhood of Union Carpenters as a required element of every qualified bid.*

The greater good

Meaning: As between two competing interests, the one which most benefits the broader group of people.

Example: *The radicals and racists, comprising the coterie, rationalized that burning down shops and stealing from helpless merchants was fully justified by what they shamelessly referred to as being "the greater good."*

The greatest/best thing since sliced bread

Meaning: Hyperbole for something that seems to be spectacularly favorable.

Example: *I'm telling you, Beth, this thing—they call it the "Hula Hoop"—is the greatest thing since sliced bread, and you'll love it!*

Great minds think alike

Meaning: A patting-oneself-on-the-back type compliment to another person or persons, to the effect that the other person's idea or reasoning is not only good and correct, but it is the same as or similar to the idea or reasoning of the person doing the compliment.

Example: *The trial lawyer had the Judge in his pocket as soon as he commented, "Your Honor, great minds think alike and what I was about to say, you just said it even better!"*

Greek to me

Meaning: A description which for some reason is not understood due to being too technical or otherwise unfamiliar.

Example: *When the speaker described the inner-workings of a bankruptcy law practice, it was all Greek to me and I decided to refer-out any bankruptcy cases that came my way.*

Greener pastures

Meaning: A person or place of more auspicious qualities, such as climate, wealth, leisure time and beauty.

Example: *Paris had been a whirlwind of excitement and cultural events for the wealthy newlyweds, but after three days they decided to move on to greener pastures for quiet times along the Cliffs of Dover.*

Green light

Meaning: Approval of a project for funding and a start date.

Example: *Finally, after more than twenty years as a writer of feature film screenplays, my script titled "Spacetime" was green lit for production by a major film studio.*

Grey area

Meaning: An in-between subject with no absolutely clear governing rules.

Example: *Blueprinting the engine by balancing parts from several different engines was a grey area in the Spec car-racing class, and Fred took full advantage of this ambiguity to produce an unusually strong engine for his Spec Miata race car.*

Grin and bear it

Meaning: Take adversity in stride and look to the future.

Example: *His dad encouraged him to grin and bear it in response to the class bully, but Jimbo Perkins decided to let his fists do the talking instead.*

Grocery list

Meaning: A mundane list of brief descriptions of things related to a task or activity.

Example: *In the second-year Evidence class, a skeptical student confronted the professor, "You mean to say we gotta learn some grocery list of exceptions to the hearsay rule?"*

Guilty as sin

Meaning: That someone is obviously, indisputably and undeniably responsible for immoral or seriously illegal conduct.

Example: *The young rascal was guilty as sin, but his Third-Grade teacher decided to cut him a break—provided that the boy return the brand-new kickball by high noon tomorrow.*

Gun-shy

Meaning: Fearful of difficult situations.

Example: *The veteran attorney was gun-shy about taking on another defendant in a criminal prosecution, after the Judge in his prior trial had been so outrageously biased in favor of the prosecution.*

Gunboat diplomacy

Meaning: Negotiating from a position of strength, ultimatums and threats of serious consequences.

Example: *The President wisely employed gunboat diplomacy in dealing with terrorists in Somalia.*

A hail Mary

> **Meaning:** A desperate tactic of last resort, when no more conservative action is capable of succeeding.
>
> **Example:** *The candy shop simply couldn't compete with price-points set by big-box stores, so as a hail Mary, it decided to give out free samples, asking in return simply a pledge to make a purchase within thirty days.*

Hair today, gone tomorrow

> **Meaning:** A tongue-in-cheek reference to losing one's hair.
>
> **Example:** *When the hairstylist mentioned some hair loss in the crown of his head, he laughed and replied, "Hair today, gone tomorrow."*

Half a mind

> **Meaning:** A serious consideration of doing something.
>
> **Example:** *I've got half a mind to buy an all-winter ski pass, just for the sake of having it available when I'm able to ski again.*

Half-baked

Meaning: Something that is only completed part way, as if that would be enough.

Example: *The Vice President covered his face with his two hands, looked up and warned the Junior Executive, "Don't ever even think about bringing me some half-baked marketing plan again."*

Hand in glove

Meaning: Two things that work closely together or in sync.

Example: *Having good credit goes hand in glove with spending within one's means.*

Hand-over-fist

Meaning: A lot now and more coming.

Example: *Once he started selling online and delivering in heat-retention packaging, the meat pie baker was making money hand-over-fist.*

Hands are tied

Meaning: One's actions and options are constrained or inhibited due to some external policy or edict.

Example: *Son, I'd like to help you here, I sure enough would, but you gotta understand that my hands are tied seein' as how you entered the store with the intent to steal, and that there is burglary, plain and simple.*

Hands down

Meaning: Without doubt.

Example: *The blonde was hands down the cuter of the two, but the brunette was clearly more fun.*

Hand to mouth

Meaning: Surviving on a budget such that whatever money comes in, is almost immediately spent on basic living expenses.

Example: *The ex-nurse was unemployed and obviously living hand to mouth.*

The handwriting/writing is on the wall

Meaning: Something is well known and unambiguous.

Example: *After the Blazers' closer, Cole Harding, loaded the bases on three straight base-on-balls, the writing was on the wall that he was out and the young Southpaw was in to save the game.*

Hanging on by a thread

Meaning: Barely surviving in an activity (even one's own life), which could be lost at any moment.

Example: *Grandpa was hanging on by a thread, but he still cracked a joke when he saw mom enter the hospital room.*

Hangs in the balance

Meaning: Something is dependent on the outcome of something else.

Example: *While their appeal of the Judgment against them*

was pending, our future financial survival was hanging in the balance.

A happy camper

Meaning: A light-hearted description of someone pleased with the current state of affairs of the present activity.

Example: *Myrtle Dinglehopper was a happy camper as she sat on the shaded porch in her rocking chair, sipping a glass of cold lemonade and watching the crimson sunset.*

A hard nut to crack

Meaning: A difficult problem to resolve.

Example: *Learning to speak Japanese turned out to be a hard nut to crack, until he met the ravishing Miko Miyama, who taught him the language, one kiss at a time.*

Hard of hearing

Meaning: Hearing impaired.

Example: *Once my hard of hearing Grandma was fitted with the latest of hearing aids, she became an indomitable flibbertigibbet at the Wednesday bridge parties.*

Hard/difficult to put the toothpaste back in the tube

Meaning: Once something is said or done it is difficult if not impossible to take it back.

Example: *As much as the lawyer believed in the content of his ill-timed outburst in open Court, it was hard to put the toothpaste back in the tube, and the Judge held him in Contempt quicker than you could say lickety-split.*

Harmless as a heel hound

Meaning: An old Southern idiom for, docile and defenseless.

Example: *Now that that two-bit lawyer don't got access to them Courts no more, why he's harmless as a heel hound.*

Haste makes waste

Meaning: The most reliable path to success in a project is to take the time reasonably required and complete the project correctly the first time, with the fewest mistakes.

Example: *To save time, Scott skipped a step of splitting the case and cleaning out any chards of metal, but haste makes waste and in the first day following the engine rebuild, it self-destructed.*

Hat trick

Meaning: A mostly, but not exclusively, sports term—a threefold feat within one game; or, an exceptionally clever accomplishment.

Example: *Deputy Public Defender Vosine Williams was on a roll with a hat trick of three consecutive Not Guilty jury verdicts in federal District Court.*

Have a crack at (something)

Meaning: Try to do something.

Example: *Lemme have a crack at that mechanical bull—I used to ride horses as a kid!*

Have a heart

Meaning: A request for compassion.

Example: *The physician strongly encouraged the parents to have a heart and allow him to admit their son to the hospital for observation, if only for an overnight.*

Have a sweet tooth

Meaning: A craving for sugar in some form such as ice cream or candy.

Example: *Olaf was well-known for his sweet tooth, and interrupted his "body-transport" errand to stop in at the local candy store for a half pound of irresistible peanut brittle.*

Have a trick up (one's) sleeve

Meaning: Be in possession of undisclosed special skills, resources or knowledge which will help in the situation.

Example: *I told my son that Dad's got a trick up his sleeve, and then proceeded to pull out three coupons with a combined value of just a dollar fifty shy of paying for a large popcorn and two sodas.*

(To) have eyes for (someone)

Meaning: To be attracted physically and emotionally to another particular person.

Example: *Mary Lou whispered to her friend, "Sara, that boy over yonder, I think he's got eyes for you."*

Have (one's) fill

Meaning: To have little remaining patience for experiencing something further.

Example: *Petey Perkins was tired and hungry and had had his* *fill of listening to that old goat complain about how bronc riders drink and cuss so much.*

Have I got news for you!

Meaning: An expression used to alert one's listener to get ready for an exciting, desirable announcement.

Example: *Dad came home early from work on Friday, walked through the front door and excitedly told my mom, two sisters and me, "Have I got news for you—We're going to the water park!"*

Have (someone) in (one's) corner

Meaning: To be backed up by someone when the need arises.

Example: *I knew I was at a disadvantage being up against three adverse lawyers, but I had the facts on my side and a premiere expert in soils engineering in my corner, so I believed I'd prevail.*

Have my/your head examined

Meaning: Often stated facetiously—criticism of someone's thought process.

Example: *I made a huge mistake in trusting you and I obviously ought to have my head examined.*

Have the ear of (someone)

Meaning: Had an open channel of communication with someone.

Example: *Sure, my water polo coach in college thought I was* *holding back as a forward, but I had the ear of our hole man and he convinced the coach to try me out as point.*

Have the/an edge

Meaning: To possess an advantage of some kind.

Example: *In quick-draw, I knew I'd have an edge over Victor "the King" Robles, but the guy wanted to fight, and die, all the same.*

Have/need to wear it

Meaning: Need to openly take responsibility for one's decision, conduct, mistake or statement.

Example: *The film director took the seasoned actor aside and warned her courteously but firmly, "If you disrespect the Background actors one more time, you'll have to wear it and so help me god, I'll fire you in a New York Minute."*

Have-nots

Meaning: Lower middle class or poverty-level persons.

Example: *When I was growing up, I wasn't really aware that there were have-nots, but when I became a young lawyer, the have-nots were all around me as defendants in criminal prosecutions.*

Have (one's) work cut out

Meaning: The challenges of the job are substantial.

Example: *As a young actor, I knew I'd have my work cut out for me, but I never expected to be discriminated against for NOT being gay.*

Have your head in the clouds

Meaning: To be confused and distracted.

Example: *Mister Cowan, Johnny's 4th Grade teacher, woke him out of his daydream, stating, "Johnny, hey, do you have your head in the clouds?"*

The hay is in the barn

Meaning: The fundamental, preparatory work and training is, or has been, all accomplished.

Example: *Missy Cheng had some butterflies waiting for her name to be called for the Women's Singles badminton finals, but the hay was in the barn and she knew she could win this match, as long as she kept her focus.*

Head on the block/Head on the chopping block

Meaning: In immediate jeopardy of being fired, criticized, disciplined or persecuted for something.

Example: *Seven-year-old Eunice insisted on selling lemonade on the corner with her younger brother, Richie, but her head was on the block with their mom if the police showed up again because of no business license.*

Head over heels

Meaning: A profound infatuation.

Example: *In 3rd Grade I was head over heels in love with a bright young girl in my class named Joann Washum, but I was way too shy to tell her.*

Heads I win, tails you lose

Meaning: The way this is set up, either way you do it, I will prevail.

Example: *The morally corrupt Jurist leaned back in his oversized chair and scoffed at defendant's attorney, "You're in a trap, Counselor, and believe me when I tell you—heads I win, tails you lose."*

Heads up/head-to-head

Meaning: In poker, where only two people are playing, one against the other.

Example: *They were head-to-head at the final table, and the winner would take home a cool million in cash.*

Heads up

Meaning: Alert.

Example: *I want everyone heads up at the pitch meeting this afternoon, if for no other reason than that each of your jobs depends on it.*

Heads up

Meaning: A status update on some situation or project.

Example: *Mister Denlinger, thanks for the heads up, and I mean it, 'cause I wanna make sure no one disturbs your team during its stay with us.*

Heads will roll

Meaning: People will be punished because of what has happened.

Example: *When CEO Arthur P. Footleman read over the Quarterly Financials deposited on his desk, he stood up, tossed the reports across the room and vociferously exclaimed, "Heads will roll for this, heads will roll!"*

Healthy as a horse

Meaning: Strong and feeling good with no serious medical issues.

Example: *This morning it was amazing—I felt healthy as a horse, stretched for a while, did a raft of pushups and sit-ups, rode my bike for about 10 miles and played two-hours of badminton later in the day!*

Hear a pin drop

Meaning: The surroundings are exceedingly quiet.

Example: *At that very moment in the play, when the lovers were about to kiss, you could hear a pin drop in the theatre, as their whispers spoke wonders of the depth of their love.*

Heard it through the grapevine

Meaning: Learned of something from comments passed around by various people in the know.

Example: *The lawyer dodged the question, stating to the Media that he'd heard it through the grapevine, not from any specific source.*

Heart of gold

Meaning: A deep and abiding loyalty, concern and compassion.

Example: *For once, I instinctively trusted this candidate for City Council, as I strongly sensed she had a heart of gold and would work tirelessly for the greater good as a City Councilperson.*

Heart-to-heart talk

Meaning: A one-on-one discussion on matters of substantial concern.

Example: *When I was first about to drive away to college, my father took me aside for a heart-to-heart talk and advised me, incredibly, that it was best to avoid sexual relations until after marriage.*

Heavens to Betsy

Meaning: A somewhat antiquated, but still, a cute expression of surprise.

Example: *Cynthia Croprock took one look at her granddaughter's lavender Prom dress and exclaimed, "Heavens to Betsy, that is perfectly stunning!"*

Heavy-handed

Meaning: Actions exhibiting little if any subtlety or refinement.

Example: *The guitarist certainly knew the overall structure of the complicated classical guitar piece, Two Guitars, but the presentation was decidedly heavy-handed, gauche and disappointing.*

Hedge (one's) bets

Meaning: Take advance precautions to mitigate damages in the event of a failed activity.

Example: *We wanted to take the cruise, but to hedge our bets in the event the cruise was cancelled for any reason, we had hotel and flight reservations for Pagosa Springs, Colorado as well.*

Hell-bent

Meaning: Absolutely and adamantly committed to a particular action.

Example: *Hal was Hell-bent on leaving San Felipe, Mexico, with all the crashes and injuries that went down on that ill-fated, off-road motorcycle trip.*

(Going to) Hell in a hand-basket

Meaning: Rapidly becoming an out-of-control disaster.

Example: *The party started off peacefully enough, until the Shinpaigoto Motorcycle Club arrived, and it thereafter went to Hell in a hand-basket.*

Herding cats

Meaning: Rounding up people who scatter and are not interested in being rounded up.

Example: *Confining protesters to the town square was like herding cats, and before you knew it, the crowd had splintered off to City Hall.*

Here today, gone tomorrow

Meaning: Some things are ephemeral.

Example: *I know, I was flush yesterday, but here today, gone tomorrow, I'm all tapped out today.*

Here we go again

Meaning: Something similar has happened before and now, again.

Example: *When Hakeem "Easter Bunny" Thomas entered the Courtroom with his lawyer, his personal assistant and his bodyguard, the Judge muttered to himself, "Here we go again," and called the case of Centennial Broadcasting Corporation versus The Rapper known as Easter Bunny.*

He who laughs last, laughs best

Meaning: Revenge for being previously hurt or otherwise wronged is better than making the first move.

Example: *He left her at the restaurant to pay the tab, but he who laughs last laughs best as she paid the bill plus a handsome tip with the credit card he had given her earlier in the day to buy gas.*

(He/she wouldn't) hurt a fly

Meaning: They are harmless.

Example: *Vanessa reassured Sylvia that Ted was a true gentleman and wouldn't hurt a fly and based on that reference, Sylvia said "Yes!" to Ted's invitation.*

(Neither) hide nor hair

Meaning: No trace of something.

Example: *We searched far and wide but there was neither hide nor hair of anyone even remotely resembling actor Jack Forbes at the famed Avocado Festival.*

High and mighty

Meaning: A derogatory term for egotistical, condescending character traits.

Example: *The landlord was despicable in his efforts to raise rents by over 35% of the full rental rate, in a single year, and his corresponding high and mighty attitude didn't help one bit in the already-sketchy Landlord-Tenant relations.*

High and tight

Meaning: A baseball term—placement of a "brushback" pitch, thrown up near a batter's face, in order to motivate him to refrain from "crowding" the plate (home plate).

Example: *Reginal Reynolds threw a 94-miles per hour fastball high and tight at Barracuda's Shortstop, and that cleared the benches of both clubs.*

High as a kite

Meaning: Very intoxicated and impaired.

Example: *The sixteen-year-old was high as a kite on rum and coke by the time police arrived at the single-vehicle crash scene.*

(Living) high on the hog

Meaning: Spending lavishly for an exorbitantly excessive lifestyle.

Example: *Sure, we were living high on the hog, until the money ran out and the electricity and water were shut off.*

High-handed

Meaning: Morally deficient.

Example: *She didn't appreciate her own lawyer's high-handed treatment of the tenants, and decided to override his dictate that they vacate the premises by noon on Tuesday.*

Highway robbery

Meaning: Setting a price that is so excessive that it seems like the buyer is being cheated.

Example: *Prices were sky-rocketing all over town and selling apples for $9.00 per pound was nothing short of highway robbery.*

Hill of beans

Meaning: Nothing serious or significant.

Example: *Clearly it was a political miscue asking that homeless pay a use tax for living on the street, but after the requisite apologies, the incident didn't amount to a hill of beans.*

Hindsight is 20-20

Meaning: When looking back on something that has already concluded, it is always easier to determine the best path forward, compared to making decisions in real time, under pressure, in the heat of the moment.

Example: *While it's true that she slapped me—hard—after I kissed her on the first date, hindsight's 20-20 and without hesitation I'd do it again!*

His bark is worse than his bite

Meaning: He may seem tough or dangerous, but he's basically well-behaved and harmless.

Example: *The Mayor appeared formidable enough, with his* *jiu-jitsu and kung fu background, but truth be told, his bark is worse than his bite.*

Hit a nerve

Meaning: Touch on a particularly sensitive subject to someone.

Example: *When the speaker suggested that all unvaccinated persons must be confined to what amount to concentration camps, it hit a nerve and became clear to me that we had to fight against this unparalleled tyranny.*

Hit and miss

Meaning: Unpredictable.

Example: *No matter how good a performance felt in an audition—because of the unknown factors of what they were looking for, it was always hit and miss in actually booking the job.*

Hit below the belt

Meaning: Acting in a manner that would be considered "dirty" or against the rules or informal code of conduct.

Example: *When she threatened to reveal Maurice's homosexual activities, he knew that she had hit him below the belt, but he countered by uncovering some very kinky websites Penelope had recently frequented.*

Hit home

Meaning: Have an emotional effect sufficient to influence.

Example: *When Tommy heard about his friend's loss, it really* *hit home and he couldn't wait to see his own mom again to say he loved and appreciated her.*

Hit it outta the park

Meaning: Often, but not exclusively a baseball expression—to hit a baseball for a "home run," where, without defensive error, the batter scores after hitting the pitched ball.

Example: *Bill hit it outta the park with his ad campaign presentation that emphasized the medical benefits of a solid night's sleep on the Narzoxsan mattress.*

Hit it with your best shot

Meaning: Do your very best in this attempt.

Example: *After the shiftless carney told the precocious 7-year old girl to "Hit it with your best shot," she did just that and won herself a Kewpie doll.*

Hit-list

Meaning: Identification of certain targeted persons or things.

Example: *The local fire station was on his hit-list, as he campaigned for a City Council seat in the 4th District.*

Hit or miss

Meaning: Something that could either be right or wrong, appropriate or inappropriate, and successful or unsuccessful.

Example: *The night rescue mission was going to be hit or miss and the security team knew it, but the hostage was the 12-year-old* *daughter of our Ambassador to Afghanistan and to the man, they were all in.*

Hit rock bottom

Meaning: A state of existence which is the lowest one can go regarding a particular set of adverse conditions.

Example: *The soap opera character, Wes Taylor, hit rock bottom when his guilt over the accidental death of his infant daughter led him to crack cocaine abuse and homelessness.*

Hit the books

Meaning: Study something through reading and research.

Example: *The first-year law student hit the books six to seven days a week during the school year because she realized that this legal education formed the very foundation of the rest of her life.*

Hit the deck

Meaning: Quickly lie down on the ground or floor.

Example: *When shots rang out at the elementary school, most of the teachers and students hit the deck, but one teacher, Victoria Applebaum, went hunting for the gunman.*

Hit the ground running

Meaning: Continue the pursuit without undue delay and without holding back.

Example: *The NASA engineers hit the ground running when they received word that the International Space Station had an atmospheric leak that was growing larger and more ominous by the hour.*

Hit the hay/sack

Meaning: To retire to bed for sleep.

Example: *After three hours of almost constant badminton games, I was dead-tired and soon after dinner I hit the sack for the night.*

Hit the jackpot

Meaning: An unexpected event of receiving something exceptionally valuable compared with the cost or effort.

Example: *When I first met my wife and she smiled softly, I knew I'd hit the jackpot for sure.*

Hit the mark

Meaning: Do something that is exactly on point and successful.

Example: *The general contractor hit the mark with his framing subcontractor's work, and next up to bat were the electrical contractors.*

Hit the nail on the head

Meaning: Communicate a point that is exactly correct.

Example: *Mister Abernathy hit the nail on the head when he asked the City Council why the mask-mandate was still in place despite the fact that there was not a single case of COVID-19 in any hospital within the City.*

Hit the road

Meaning: Leave for a destination.

Example: *It was O-dark-thirty when we hit the road for our Saturday surf trip.*

Hit the sack
Meaning: Go to sleep.
Example: *It was 2:45 in the morning when I finished the latest Harlan County P.T.A. novel and finally hit the sack.*

Hit (one's) stride
Meaning: For a person to be knowledgeable, experienced and productive in his or her avocation.
Example: *America's hopeful, Lisa Chang, hit her stride at the Badminton World Championships in Innsbruck, Austria, defeating Germany's Karin Struple, 21-18, 21-6.*

Hobson's choice
Meaning: A mere *illusion* of free choice where in actuality, only one option is offered.
Example: *The stoic billionaire sat with his advisors, attorneys and business associates across the conference table and presented a classic Hobson's choice to the young I.T. entrepreneur—sign the contract now or get nothing.*

Hog heaven
Meaning: An exceedingly happy state of mind.
Example: *The pinch-hitting college senior was in hog heaven after she hit a walk-off home run in the bottom of the seventh.*

Hold all the aces

Meaning: Have all the advantages in a particular area of activity.

Example: *Considering his water polo and martial arts background, this lifeguard held all the aces in any struggle for control with a drowning swimmer.*

Hold down the fort

Meaning: To undertake all of the usual steps to maintain status quo at work or home.

Example: *When her parents left for a weekend in Palm Springs, Simone's dad told her to hold down the fort at home for a couple of days, and she was true to her word.*

Hold (one's) feet to the fire

Meaning: Apply threatened or actual pressure as a forceful incentive to someone.

Example: *The Dean wasn't receptive to your suggestion of initiating a Pharmaceutical-Consumer Law class for the Fall Semester, but if I hold his feet to the fire over his recent arrest for pornography possession, he'll likely capitulate.*

(To be left) holding the bag

Meaning: Abandoned by your cohorts under incriminating personal circumstances.

Example: *Alvin mistakenly assumed he could trust Darnell and Lionel in the burglary, but they left him holding the bag and they fled the scene just before the law arrived.*

Hold (one's) own

Meaning: Act or operate in a comparably-successful manner.

Example: *The CPA was able to hold her own in the courtroom, despite the fact that she had no prior forensic accounting experience.*

(To) hold out an olive branch

Meaning: To offer a truce or cessation of hostilities.

Example: *It's true that the CEO held out an olive branch to the careless Accounting Manager, but it was on condition that the Manager be demoted to an Assistant Manager position with a corresponding pay cut.*

Hold the phone

Meaning: Wait for a moment.

Example: *Hey, hey buddy boy, just hold the phone now, 'cause I didn't do what you think I did.*

Hold your horses

Meaning: Hang on and stop for a moment.

Example: *If you would hold your horses for just a doggone minute, I would explain to you exactly why I'm here in your bedroom with your wife.*

Hold your tongue

Meaning: Refrain from revealing one's thoughts.

Example: *As an experienced button-man, I was obligated, out of* *instinct for self-preservation, to hold my tongue when the mark was speakin' out against my boss.*

Hole in one

Meaning: A golfing term— during a game or match, when from the tee box a player hits a golf ball which then drops into the "cup."

Example: *At the par three, 7th hole that day, any player who managed to hit a hole in one would win a brand-new Ford Mustang convertible.*

Hollow victory

Meaning: Winning where the cause of competition was not a particularly favorable one or where the victory did not particularly advance one's overall interests.

Example: *The job action was successful in removing the minimum education requirement for delivery drivers, but it was a hollow victory considering that the company was losing business and several drivers were laid off.*

Holy smoke!

Meaning: An exclamation of surprise and astonishment!

Example: *Holy smoke, I didn't realize it was so late—turn on Channel 9!*

Home again, home again, Finnegan

Meaning: Home is a great place to be again.

Example: *The Brewster Family had such an exhilarating outing at the Reynolds Company annual picnic, it was home again,* *home again, Finnegan with all of the kids falling asleep on the way.*

Home away from home

Meaning: A place that is not actually home, but feels almost like it is.

Example: *The Mexican restaurant, Don Carlos, and its exceptionally cordial staff, gradually became the writer's home away from home, as he went there not only to eat dinner but also to escape from his computer.*

Home is where the heart is

Meaning: Other places may have their allure, but the favorite place is always with one's friends and family.

Example: *Although banished from their home during termite fumigation, Bob and Sally Smithers were still together in their hotel room and for them, home is where the heart is.*

Home, James

Meaning: A request to the driver to head to the speaker's place of residence.

Example: *Sherrie and I had had such an awesome time at dinner and the movies, and when we got to my car, I let her drive and told her, "Home, James!"*

Home sweet home

Meaning: Coming home always has a special feeling of safety, security and good memories.

Example: *Returning from a three-week sojourn to her mother's* birthplace of Seoul, Korea, Teresa commented to herself, "Home sweet home" as she stepped inside her residence.*

Honest as the day is long

Meaning: A trustworthy person of integrity.

Example: *Virginia Peabody is as honest as the day is long and I would trust her to bring in accurate vote counts, regardless of the winning and losing parties.*

The honest truth/The god's honest truth

Meaning: Without the slightest holding back from all the pertinent facts.

Example: *Okay, fine, I'm gonna tell you the god's honest truth—your daughter and I have had a relationship since she was sixteen.*

Honor among thieves

Meaning: Even criminals have a loose affinity with implied loyalty, honesty and fair dealing among crooks.

Example: *If there were ever an instance of honor among thieves, it is when a Social Media company, a State government and a Pharmaceutical company circle the wagons to withstand scrutiny over a series of vaccine-related deaths.*

Hook, line and sinker

Meaning: The fabricated story, in all its details, is believed.

Example: *After sentencing on the lesser charge, defendant Gonzales confided to his attorney, "Hey homie, they bought that phony story I give in testimony hook, line and sinker, and sorry but I couldn't tell you before it was all a big lie!"*

Hope against hope

Meaning: Be optimistic for a favorable result when there is little, if any, rational basis for believing that the outcome will be favorable.

Example: *All we could do, as a Nation, was to hope against hope that the terrorist army would not sponsor yet another suicide-bomber bombing during the evacuation.*

A horse of a different color

Meaning: A completely different situation.

Example: *If you see me as the Designated Hitter for the rest of this season, that's one thing, but if you want me to sit on the bench, just hoping to pinch hit once in a blue moon, then that's a horse of a different color and I want to be traded.*

Horse trading

Meaning: Bargaining with someone.

Example: *Sure, there was a little horse trading going on, but where is it written that you can't bargain for a better price when buying a new jet ski?*

Hot air

Meaning: Exaggerated content in speech all the way to deliberate fabrications.

Example: *This clown-of-a-Governor not only failed to stop the murderer's parole, but he was also full of hot air whenever speaking of victim's rights in a criminal prosecution.*

Hot-blooded

Meaning: Very emotional, particularly when passionate.

Example: *Sheila was an exceptionally hot-blooded woman, but I had her under control by simply asking if she would like to have some hot apple pie* a la mode.

Hot-headed

Meaning: Very emotional, particularly when angry.

Example: *This hot-headed punk was not going to single-handedly ruin the Birthday party, and I asked my daughter to send her friend home, immediately.*

A hot potato

Meaning: A controversial and even dangerous thing or event, and something to avoid.

Example: *The documentary evidence of school election irregularities was definitely a hot potato and the Editor in Chief of the Mustang Gazette student newspaper passed on the story.*

Hotter than/'an a hen house in July

Meaning: Very uncomfortably hot.

Example: *I tried to warn that it gets hotter 'an a hen house in July out here.*

Hotter than/'an a blister bug in a pepper patch

Meaning: Very uncomfortably hot.

Example: *She looked me up and down, handed me an ice-cold lemonade and said, "Well drink up, Mister, or don't you know* *that it's hotter than a blister bug in a pepper patch out here this time of year."*

Hotter than/'an a June bride in a feather bed

Meaning: Very uncomfortably hot.

Example: *The two grizzled old men looked at each other, sweatin' like there's no tomorrow and simultaneously exclaimed, "It's hotter out here than a June bride in a feather bed!"*

Hotter than/'an a two-Dollar pistol

Meaning: Very uncomfortably hot.

Example: *The five-year old boy wore his toy six-shooters and a cowboy hat, sat on his tricycle with handle-bar colored tassels, nodded his head and said to his mama, "Tell you what—it's hotter out here than a two-Dollar pistol!"*

Hotter than/'an blue blazes

Meaning: Very uncomfortably hot.

Example: *It was hotter than blue blazes in the Courtroom after the power went out, and the Court called a recess in the proceedings until 8:30 a.m. of the following day.*

Hot ticket

Meaning: Something or someone in unusually strong demand.

Example: *In her short-shorts and halter top, Lucille was definitely the hot ticket, and she knew it full well.*

Hot water

Meaning: Lots of trouble.

Example: *Our gardener was in hot water for breaking a sprinkler lead and not repairing it—but worse yet was concealing the problem with some soil and a large rock.*

Hours on end

Meaning: Several hours.

Example: *The lawyer's tedious closing arguments to the jury seemed to drone on and on, for hours on end, until the frustrated Judge piped in, "Alright counsel, now you've got exactly five more minutes to wrap it up, and I mean pronto."*

House of cards

Meaning: An organization or group, the premise of which is so contradictory, false or weak that it could fall apart literally at any moment.

Example: *By instituting a demand that every actor become vaccinated, the producers created a house of cards, revealing themselves, once and for all, as unscrupulous and power-hungry— to which, pathetically, the vast majority of members voted to bow down.*

How do you like them apples?

Meaning: A rhetorical question to convey the excitement of bad news for someone to whom he is speaking, but good news for the speaker.

Example: *Immediately prior to ejection from the ballgame* *by the Home Plate Umpire, the homerun hitter quipped to the pitcher, "How do you like them apples?"*

How does that grab you?

Meaning: What do you think about that idea?

Example: *We could tell Dad the car must have been hit in the parking lot somehow—How does that grab you?*

How long is a piece of string?

Meaning: This is a question with no clear and discernable answer.

Example: *Asked how long he believed the quarantine would last, the public official flatly replied, "How long is a piece of string?"*

Hungry as a horse

Meaning: Hungry to the point of practically starving.

Example: *After a morning of fighting 25-miles per hour headwinds on half of my eight-mile bicycling loop, I was hungry as a horse and started scouring the kitchen for food.*

Hunky-dory

Meaning: A somewhat corny way of expressing that one is great, awesome.

Example: *Teri asked little Skippy Warner how he was doing today and he smiled and replied, "I'm hunky-dory, how about you?"*

Icing on the cake

Meaning: An extra ingredient of success which was not minimally necessary but which was greatly appreciated by the victorious.

Example: *Melinda Torres found that the icing on the cake was her boyfriend's presence, at mile-12 of the marathon, cheering her on to victory.*

I didn't just fall off the turnip truck

Meaning: I have at least a normal degree of experience and knowledge on the particular subject, and I am definitely not blindly ignorant.

Example: *Floyd was not inclined to turn in his firearms in the government buy-back program, and commented to his neighbor, Jed, "I may be stupid, but I didn't just fall off the turnip truck."*

I do declare

Meaning: A Southern (of the United States) expression for, realization and even astonishment.

Example: *When the slick young lawyer knocked politely,*

Louise Williams sauntered to the front door, looked through the screen and commented, "Well, I do declare, Mister Bingham—to what do I owe the pleasure?"

I couldn't agree with you more

Meaning: I strongly agree with you.

Example: *You can stop right there because I couldn't agree with you more!*

I couldn't care less

Meaning: I don't care at all in the slightest degree.

Example: *Counselor, I really couldn't care less about the precise date on which the product was invented or conceived, but I am interested in when examples of it were first placed into commerce.*

If a pig had wings, it could fly

Meaning: If things were different, there would not be this situation, but things are not different.

Example: *Martin's rather crass father surveyed his baseball attire and advised, "If a pig had wings, it could fly, but go ahead an' see if you got any baseball skills."*

If it hit (someone) over the head

Meaning: Even with the facts and probable outcome laid out clearly and plainly.

Example: *The resilient lad wouldn't know defeat if it hit him over the head—he just never quits.*

If it looks like a duck, swims like a duck, and quacks like a duck, it's probably a duck

> **Meaning:** Things usually are what they appear to be.
>
> **Example:** *To the prosecutor's question of whether the body, with its multiple stab wounds, was a homicide victim, the coroner stated, flatly—"If it looks like a duck, swims like a duck, and quacks like a duck, it's probably a duck."*

If it's not broke, don't fix it [or] If it ain't broke, don't fix it

> **Meaning:** Meddling with operable things or situations often results in making things worse.
>
> **Example:** *The trainer strongly advised against her client doing any last minute "tweaking" of his horse, stating, "Mister Cunningham, kindly don't make any 'adjustments' to Pistol Pete before the show, 'cause if it's not broke, don't fix it."*

If the shoe fits, (one should) wear it

> **Meaning:** If something strongly seems to describe a person's character or actions, then they should accept and acknowledge that fact.
>
> **Example:** *Mortimer Paige was happy to acquiesce to the adjective of "skinflint" since if the shoe fits, he should wear it.*

If you can't stand the heat, get outta the kitchen

> **Meaning:** If the demands and pressure of the situation are too great, then they should back off and allow others to handle it.
>
> **Example:** *The insolent CEO banged his fist and warned the*

obdurate Vice President, "If you can't stand the heat, get outta of the kitchen!"

If you don't like it, (you can) lump it

Meaning: A somewhat antagonistic expression for, this is the way it is, regardless of whether it meets your approval.

Example: *She calmly turned to her husband and announced that she was, in fact, going to accept the job offer and that if he didn't like it, he could lump it.*

If you know what I mean

Meaning: An overused expression usually having no meaning at all and used simply as an exclamation point to what the speaker has said, or a sort of request for periodic or tacit agreement to what the speaker has just said, if you know what I mean.

Example: *The mofo had it comin' an' I give it to him is all, if you know what I mean.*

If worst comes to worst

Meaning: In the event that all more favorable options are unavailable.

Example: *I assured my friend that if worst comes to worst and I can't sell my condo, I'll pay him back the balance of the loan on its due date from a credit card cash advance.*

I got your six/back

Meaning: I'm here to protect you and your safety or other interests.

Example: *Homey, chu don need to worry, 'cuz I got your six man.*

Ignorance is bliss

Meaning: People who are oblivious to the truth are, at least in the short term, insulated from the stress and worry which would otherwise arise from knowledge of the actual facts.

Example: *They lived in their high-rise, luxury condominiums all but isolated from the mental illness, drug addiction, despair and homelessness on the streets below, but ignorance is bliss.*

Ill at ease

Meaning: Not comfortable with something.

Example: *Reina's father was ill at ease with her plans to travel out-of-State unaccompanied, but eventually he capitulated and wished her luck in the U-22 soccer tournament.*

I'll eat my hat

Meaning: A rhetorical exclamation for, I will be incredibly surprised.

Example: *After the debacle of last season's playoffs, if the Hughes Park Rangers make it to the Championship finals, I'll eat my hat.*

Ill-gotten gains

Meaning: Profits from an illegal or highly immoral undertaking.

Example: *Despite her destitute circumstance, Mable shunned* *her incorrigible sons and refused to accept any of their ill-gotten gains.*

I like my coffee the way I like my men

Meaning: A gay expression for, I prefer relationships with black men.

Example: *As Bob approached the demure Steven in the park, Steven countered, "Sorry, but I like my coffee the way I like my men."*

I'm all ears

Meaning: Often but not always stated sarcastically for, I'm ready to listen to anything you have to say.

Example: *When Craig Youngblood claimed to have a lot of dirt on their father, Craig's sister Beatrice sarcastically said, "I'm all ears."*

I'm down with that

Meaning: I agree with your plan and/or agree to participate in the activity.

Example: *Bass guitar laid down some notes and the rhythm guitarist commented, "I'm down with that," and worked in a cool chord progression.*

I'm your huckleberry

Meaning: To declare oneself as a friend or the right person for a task, sometimes stated sarcastically.

Example: *Immediately prior to the starting-gun blast, Alvin* *glanced at Horatio and stated, "I'm your huckleberry," then proceeded to smoke him in the footrace.*

In a fix

Meaning: Caught-up in a difficult or embarrassing predicament.

Example: *Amid rampant allegations of consumer fraud and peppered by deep distrust from his step-daughter, Spencer Silversleppin was in a fix with no way out.*

In a jam

Meaning: Caught-up in a troublesome or difficult situation

Example: *I was in a jam and I knew it, but I couldn't let my only cash-customer know or suspect it.*

In a million years

Meaning: For such an extensively long time that it will never happen.

Example: *She had tried to get Billy McAlister to notice her all school year, but in a million years he wouldn't respond since what she didn't know was that Billy is gay.*

In a pickle

Meaning: Caught-up in a difficult or embarrassing predicament.

Example: *While it's true that I was in a pickle, I was confident I could find some dirt on the private investigator who held the embarrassing photos.*

In a nutshell

Meaning: The main essential details of the topic of conversation.

Example: *In a nutshell, I'll tell you one word: Plastics—thank you for attending, everyone.*

In a pig's eye

Meaning: It's not going to happen as they think it will.

Example: *In a pig's eye I'll dismiss the case—we're here to win and win big!*

In a tight spot

Meaning: Confronted with a difficult situation.

Example: *The lone police officer was in a tight spot, with video cameras pointed in his direction and a violent offender struggling to disarm him.*

In broad daylight

Meaning: Outdoors, during the daytime hours, with excellent visibility.

Example: *The middle-aged man was arrested for indecent exposure and seven independent persons witnessed it in broad daylight.*

In cahoots

Meaning: Engaged in a conspiracy with another perpetrator.

Example: *The two women were obviously in cahoots, with Sally as the shoplifter and Melissa distracting the security detail.*

Inclement weather

Meaning: Uncomfortably and severely stormy.

Example: *The tournament organizers were faced with a forecast of inclement weather and decided to commence tomorrow's final round at 8:00 a.m., on split tees, with threesomes.*

In deep water

Meaning: In a complicated situation that is potentially dangerous.

Example: *The federal operatives knew they would be in deep water the second they forced entry to the fortified headquarters of the Chicago Outfit.*

In dribs and drabs

Meaning: A few at a time, sporadically.

Example: *The negative performance reviews came in dribs and drabs in Sam's personnel file, but the cumulative effect was to stop him from advancing in the company.*

In droves

Meaning: In waves of a lot at a time.

Example: *After his performance as "Steely Ned" in the* Under the Starlight *revival, fan mail arrived in droves for theatre-actor Ben Cousins.*

I need that like I need a hole in my/the head

Meaning: I don't need that at all.

Example: *Charles Oliphant had been fighting the Atlantic Blue Fin Tuna for the better part of an hour, when a large shark fin* *cut through the ocean surface, at which time he blurted out, "Oh, perfect, I need that like I need a hole in the head."*

In (one's) element
Meaning: Doing something that is well-within one's training and experience.
Example: *Martha Zimmerman was well within her element as she argued her first appellate case to the Court of Appeal—and won!*

In for a penny, in for a pound
Meaning: Once one participates or is otherwise involved at all, they are committed to the entire situation.
Example: *To deal with the crisis, Hank assigned the remainder of his available workers to the Drysdale Building, stating, "In for a penny, in for a pound."*

In full swing
Meaning: An activity which is underway at its optimal pace.
Example: *By the time I arrived at the bus, the Bachelor Party was in full swing, complete with two female dancers who were delighted to be aboard.*

In god we trust, but everyone else pays cash
Meaning: No one can be trusted for credit in a purchase.
Example: *The cynical hooker touched her customer's arm and remarked, "I can't extend credit, 'cause in god we trust, but everyone else pays cash."*

In high gear

Meaning: At a fast pace.

Example: *The garment workers were all in high gear when the owner arrived for his annual factory-inspection, and they feared being fired if they were to complain or to slow their feverish pace.*

In high spirits

Meaning: Enthusiastic and happy.

Example: *Buster and his buddies and all of their girlfriends were in high spirits once arriving at their San Felipe, Mexico campsite at 10:47 p.m..*

In hot water

Meaning: In trouble in some manner.

Example: *When he walked in at 3:10 a.m., it was no secret he was in hot water with his wife, who was there waiting for him.*

In light of

Meaning: Considering the fact of.

Example: *In light of all the liquor flowing that night at the Roundup Bar & Grill in Lancaster, California, we were lucky to get in and out without a fight breaking out.*

In like Flynn

Meaning: Making it into the place or activity safely and securely.

Example: *Once we had in-hand our forged invitations to the Cinco de Mayo bash, we were in like Flynn and nobody batted an eye.*

In no uncertain terms

Meaning: Explained and communicated with full and complete clarity.

Example: *The new kid at school let it be known in no uncertain terms that he would neither be bullied nor tolerate anyone else to be bullied in his presence.*

In one ear and out the other

Meaning: The message was not listened to with any level of attention and comprehension.

Example: *We tried to warn the President of the multitude of risks raised by an open-borders policy, but it was apparently in one ear and out the other.*

In one piece

Meaning: Without injury.

Example: *Manuel Jiménez was happy to walk through the front door of his home in one piece, having just been involved in a gang war and having lost four of his homies.*

In (someone's) pocket

Meaning: Controlled by someone due to unethical payoffs.

Example: *The hospitals were in the pharmaceutical's pocket, and were manipulated like puppets on strings.*

Ins and outs

Meaning: The essential details in understanding a particular environment, task or job.

Example: *As an experienced litigator of over 40 years, I knew* *the ins and outs of Family Law proceedings, and what I didn't know, I could find out through my research tools.*

In (someone's) shoes

Meaning: From the point of view or perspective of another person in their particular circumstances.

Example: *Twenty years as a prosecutor, including nine years as head of the Juvenile Division made it very difficult, if not impossible, for me to step into a liberal's shoes in giving greater attention to rehabilitation and "second chances" in juvenile justice proceedings.*

Inside scoop

Meaning: An insider's perspective and institutional knowledge.

Example: *Bobby had the inside scoop on the Winnipeg Fliers, having played Left Forward for them for three years, and was happy to pass on key tips to his new team, the Toronto Wizards.*

In so many words

Meaning: Paraphrasing, to capture the essential aspects of what was said.

Example: *Renaldo Perez explained to the school Vice Principal that Jesse Salinas, in so many words, had threatened to beat the snot out of him after school.*

In spades

Meaning: And even then, some more; and more than that.

Example: *Once Pepe called out Jonathan to stop moving while*

Pepe was putting, Jonathan was committed more than ever to defeat Pepe, in spades.

In stitches

Meaning: Laughing hard or uncontrollably.

Example: *In the movie, when the really fat guy sat down on the skinny guy, I was in stitches so bad that I actually fell out of my seat onto the aisle.*

In store

Meaning: Within the current inventory.

Example: *I was so excited to try out the new car-racing game, on the day of its release I went over to the local mall to see if the computer game place had it in store.*

In store for (someone)

Meaning: Something about to happen or be said to someone.

Example: *When I was called into my supervisor's office, I thought I knew exactly what was in store for me, but I was surprised to hear her compliment my recent work.*

In the bag

Meaning: An assured result, secured by prior action or announcement.

Example: *Acceptance to Pepperdine University, School of Law was in the bag now that he had secured a letter of recommendation from the Chief Justice of the United States Supreme Court.*

In the ballpark

Meaning: Within the general parameters of something.

Example: *I didn't need to know the exact price for the cost of converting my Miata to a Spec Miata racecar, and all I was looking for was a reliable figure in the ballpark.*

In the black

Meaning: Having greater income than overall expenses and a positive net worth.

Example: *Oliver had battled most of his life to be solidly in the black, but with the sale of Wellington Arms Estate and acquisition of the robust RGY Bearing & Power Transmission Company, he was financially secure at last.*

In the can

Meaning: The project or a portion of the project is completed and saved.

Example: *The film project,* High & Mighty, *was right on schedule and by the third day of principal photography, we had fully 10 pages of our script in the can.*

In the cards

Meaning: Within the realm of a reasonably likely outcome.

Example: *While Mickey couldn't promise me a role with definite certainty, he did describe how he knew my work—the quality of my work—and that a supporting role for me in his next film was clearly in the cards.*

In the clear

Meaning: Absolved of responsibility for something bad.

Example: *After my mother found cookie crumbs in and around my dog's mouth, I was in the clear for invading the kitchen for cookies—but Simone was in the doghouse.*

In the dark

Meaning: Uninformed.

Example: *In order to render escape more difficult, the soldiers kept their prisoners in the dark about the prison camp layout and exact location.*

In the doghouse

Meaning: In a bad situation because of doing something about which another person, typically a family member, is angry.

Example: *When Jimbo arrived late to his 7-year-old daughter's piano recital, he knew full well he was in the doghouse, but afterwards he took Kristi and her little girlfriends for ice cream, and all was forgiven.*

In the driver's seat

Meaning: In control of the situation.

Example: *Once the film director had secured "final cut" control over the film, "Deep State," he was in the driver's seat, so long as he wasn't fired for cause.*

In the face of (something)

Meaning: Under and as affected by the circumstance of something.

Example: *In the face of a monumental failure to acquire meaningful intelligence on the enemy's battle-preparedness, the General devised a plan which grossly underestimated the obstacles to success.*

In the hole

Meaning: In debt or having spent more than income received on the particular project.

Example: *By the end of the first month after buying my house, I was in the hole nearly $25,000 for needed home improvements such as fencing, flooring, window covering, kitchen appliances and an HVAC system.*

In the know

Meaning: Someone situated or experienced in such a manner as to be particularly informed in a particular subject matter.

Subject: *Keith Winterploffen was clearly in the know when it came to applying all-purpose mud to each of the wallboard joints and corners.*

In the limelight

Meaning: The focus of positive attention and admiration.

Example: *Little Chrissy Stevens loved to act and make short* *videos, and often found herself in the limelight throughout Social Media.*

In the long run

Meaning: Over a relatively lengthy period of time.

Example: *Jimbo Hornsuckle had started his stunt motorcycle career late, in his early 30s, but discovered in the long run that his exceptional talent would lead to financial success.*

In the loop

Meaning: Within the group or category of people who would be receiving information on the activity.

Example: *Bernice Tatiana was not the highest rung on the Embassy ladder, but as a State Department official, she was clearly in the loop when it came to the weekly intelligence briefing.*

In the making

Meaning: The project has commenced but is on-going and not yet completed.

Example: *Urs Kurth was an alpine ski champion in the making and had outpaced all of his coaches by age 13.*

In the palm of (one's) hand

Meaning: In close and present control of something.

Example: *Ned had the election as County Coroner in the palm of his hand, until his medical license was precipitously revoked for fraudulent medical degree documentation.*

In the pink

Meaning: In peak spirits and an excellent state of overall health.

Example: *Fred Tinderhooper had fully recovered from the snake bite and was in the pink once again.*

In the pipe/pipeline

Meaning: Within the course of activity leading toward completion.

Example: *The savvy personal injury lawyer had over one hundred cases in the pipeline and was settling or resolving by litigation nearly fifteen cases each and every month.*

In the public eye

Meaning: Due to circumstances, viewed and followed by the public at large.

Example: *Randolph Hollengale, III, heir to the Hollengale mining and oil exploration interests, was almost constantly in the public eye, and at times it tended to cramp his style with the ladies.*

In the red

Meaning: Owing or spending more than assets or income.

Example: *She was aware of his lavish lifestyle and the copious gifts being showered upon her; what she did not know was that he was deeply in the red and that this façade could not last long.*

In the same boat

Meaning: Under very similar circumstances.

Example: *The racetrack was exceptionally slippery with the pouring rain, but all of the drivers were in the same boat—no pun intended—and I just had to try to stay focused, stay fast and stay on course.*

In the thick of it
Meaning: Well within the process of the event; in contention.
Example: *With his Eagle on the 8th Hole, Edgar Wesson was in the thick of it for the tournament win.*

In the trenches
Meaning: At the forefront of dealing with a controversy or fight.
Example: *He knew from the start exactly what it was like to be in the trenches of an automotive National ad campaign.*

In the wind
Meaning: The person has gone away to some unknown location.
Example: *The writer's wife assumed he would be working in his study, but when she brought him cookies and milk, she discovered that he was in the wind.*

In the zone
Meaning: Mentally focused, effective and efficient.
Example: *The young shortstop, Jimmy-John Johnston, was definitely in the zone as Willy banged a rocket-shot towards Left Field, which Jimmy-John caught on the fly.*

Into the blue

    Meaning: Completely vanished or lost into some unknown space or time.

    Example: *One moment, the UFO was crossing into the Bermuda Triangle and then it disappeared into the blue, as if it had never existed.*

Into thin air

    Meaning: Without a trace.

    Example: *Once my wife—My Wife!—got ahold of our credit card, our "available credit" disappeared into thin air.*

Irish twins

    Meaning: Siblings born within twelve months of each other.

    Example: *Gigi and Nicki were adorable and quite difficult to tell apart, not unlike many other Irish twins.*

Ironed out

    Meaning: Resolved.

    Example: *The wifey and I ironed out our differences over a glass of Chablis and a deliciously prepared, mustard-glazed salmon with summer corn, peas and tomatoes.*

Irons in the fire

    Meaning: Resources which are in development.

    Example: *When my girl threatened to start seeing other guys, apparently, she didn't realize how many irons in the fire I had at the drop of a hat.*

In (one's) wheelhouse

Meaning: An area of one's greatest skills.

Example: *Developing a comedic commercial for milk products was right in Kay's wheelhouse, considering that before becoming a marketing professional, she grew up on a dairy farm.*

In your blood

Meaning: Almost as if one was born to do such an activity well.

Example: *I was a good ballplayer myself at his age and to boost his confidence, I assured my son Frankie that baseball was in his blood and that he could play at a championship level if he applied himself.*

In your face

Meaning: Uncomfortably close.

Example: *Officer McClusky's gonna get right in your face if you keep raising your voice to him, so please, calm down.*

It could go either way

Meaning: A situation which could easily become favorable or unfavorable for one side or outcome.

Example: *The Doubles finals of the annual Cornville, Arizona, Cornhole Championships could go either way, as each team had won past Championships.*

It goes against the grain

Meaning: Something that is averse to one's inclinations or morals.

Example: *Having owned and cared for horses in a relatively mild climate, it went against the grain to turn horses out into the mountain for the winter, but if that's what is customary in Northern Montana, then so be it.*

It has your/my name on it

Meaning: Something that seems perfectly suited to one's tastes or skills.

Example: *My girlfriend, Freida Oppenhuizen, took a fancy to a beautiful sunhat, so I told her, "It has your name on it, sweetie," and I purchased it straight away.*

It is what it is

Meaning: Something that has already occurred which cannot be changed and simply is what it appears on its face to be.

Example: *The Reynoso Rounders are short-handed for the finals of the Men's 55+, High-Arc Softball Championship, but it is what it is and they'll have to lay it all on the line tonight.*

It's a Catch-22

Meaning: A situation where each avenue of resolution or escape is blocked by opposite and seemingly contradictory moves.

Example: *It's a Catch-22 in an audition where the Casting Director is way over the top in a very distracting way, but to correct her would be a complete disaster.*

It's a drop in the bucket

Meaning: In the big picture of things, it is a very small factor.

Example: *The gratification for this bit of generosity is monumental for me, and the cost is truly a drop in the bucket.*

It's all smoke and mirrors

Meaning: It's intended to be a confusing array of deception.

Example: *When you think about a policy of actual "open borders," you realize how little you really know and that maybe it's all smoke and mirrors.*

It's an albatross around my/your neck

Meaning: It is a substantial burden that is continuing to hold one back or drag one down.

Example: *The massive credit card debt Jim Cantrell had accumulated in improving his ranch became an albatross around his neck that he couldn't quite shake.*

It's a new ballgame

Meaning: This has become an entirely different situation now.

Example: *Now that he finally got out of heavy debt, his fixed income is more than adequate and it's a new ballgame for him in the dating world.*

It's a numbers game

Meaning: This is an activity where success normally depends on a high volume of opportunities.

Example: *The talented actress wasn't booked on her callback, but she knows that it's a numbers game and is looking forward to the next audition.*

It's a wrap

Meaning: The activity, particularly as to a film shoot, is completed.

Example: *After the cameraman checked the gate, following the fifth take of the Martini Shot, the famed film director motioned to the First Assistant Director, who called out, "It's a wrap!"*

It's been real

Meaning: An expression said to another person when parting company, indicating that it has been good spending time with them; but sometimes expressed sarcastically to mean the opposite.

Example: *When my buddy from Long Beach was ready to drive back, I laughed, gave him a fist bump and told him, "It's been real."*

It's déjà vu all over again

Meaning: It's the same situation repeating itself.

Example: *Brittney was astonished at the bad luck of running into her ex-boyfriend a second time on her Tijuana vacation, and she whispered to her girlfriends, "It's déjà vu all over again—he's right over there!"*

It's getting out of hand

Meaning: It's beginning to become a bigger problem that

may be beyond one's ability to control.

Example: *Initially, he believed he could handle doing business with the Cartel, but lately it's been getting out of hand, with his employees threatened with violence.*

It's none of your business

Meaning: It is confidential and you should not ask for that information.

Example: *When asked by the impertinent clerk whether he had proof of his vaccinations, his terse reply was a simple, "It's none of your business."*

It's not my cup of tea

Meaning: It's not my preferred thing or activity.

Example: *As strategies were discussed among the itinerant miscreants, the idea was floated of walking in armed through the bank's front door, but the ringleader responded, "I'm sorry but it's not my cup of tea to engage in a daytime assault."*

It's not over, 'til it's over

Meaning: It's not resolved yet and is still subject to change, until the very end.

Example: *Shaking from exhaustion, shivering with cold, and strongly considering quitting, the 16-year-old, long-distance water skier contemplated the remaining eleven miles and found his motivation, "It's not over, 'til it's over; it's not over, 'til it's over."*

It's not rocket science

> **Meaning:** Stated somewhat sarcastically that it is a relatively easy or simple task or explanation.
>
> **Example:** *Explaining the process of analyzing and answering real estate computation questions, the tutor urged on his student, "Victor, it's not rocket science, but it does involve math and you must use fundamental principles of algebra to arrive at the correct answers."*

It's your funeral

> **Meaning:** If you do what you're planning on doing, and if it falls apart or goes wrong, then it's only you who will suffer the consequences.
>
> **Example:** *It's very simple—if you choose to gamble everything in the cryptocurrency market, then it's your funeral if and when it all goes south.*

It takes two to tango

> **Meaning:** This isn't something where one person alone could create this problem, and responsibility or blame must be shared with any other participants.
>
> **Example:** *When the idiotic feud erupted between the kitty corner residents, Jed and Wilma decided that since it takes two to tango, they would end it by disengaging completely from their neighbor.*

It was pumping

> **Meaning:** A surfing term for, the ocean waves were consistently very sizable.

Example: *As they crested the hill overlooking Upper Trestles, the four surfers started whooping and hollering because, dude, it was pumping, big time.*

It was sick

Meaning: The situation or event was fantastic.

Example: *The Wedge was cresting at 20-feet, with surfers, boogie boarders and bodysurfers swarming the water—I mean it was sick, bra.*

It will all come out in the wash

Meaning: As details of the situation are revealed, we will see a full and accurate picture of the controversy.

Example: *The Finance Committee had lost count of who had donated what to the Lowell Elementary PTA general fund, but since they retained receipts, they knew it would all come out in the wash once a full accounting was created.*

I've got your number

Meaning: I understand how you function, operate or act and I can defeat you.

Example: *As the Singles badminton match commenced, I looked at my opponent, whose game I knew very well, and thought to myself, "I've got your number," and proceeded to beat him in straight games.*

I've had it with (someone/something)

Meaning: An exasperated expression of profound distaste for a particular thing, activity, person or persons, due to adverse past experiences.

Example: *The insults and innuendo have been so pervasive and repugnant that honestly, I've* had *it with that woman and will never play badminton with her again.*

I've never done this before

Meaning: A gay expression used to feign inexperience and naivety, but where the truth is that the speaker is very experienced in what is about to happen.

Example: *As the two, rather effeminate, men slipped beneath the sheets, Marcos whispered, "I've never done this before," and softly laughed.*

Ivory tower

Meaning: A place or status of book-learning unaccompanied by actual, real-world experience.

Example: *These ivory tower pundits, in their shiny suits and porcelain teeth, have no clue what life in the hood is really like.*

I wasn't born yesterday

Meaning: I have been around long enough to know and understand a great deal about the particular subject at hand.

Example: *Just stop right there with your "explanation" on why I gotta pay for your fender, 'cause listen up—I wasn't born yesterday, is all I'm sayin'.*

I won't take "no" for an answer

Meaning: Usually stated in friendship for, I will not accept your negative reply and I insist that you allow me to help or otherwise entertain you as I have suggested.

Example: *Look, we're going to Catalina Island for the afternoon and I won't take "no" for an answer.*

I wouldn't give him/her the time of day

Meaning: I will do nothing whatsoever to respond to, or to otherwise assist, that person.

Example: *Belinda Conners, of all people, wants me to help her prep for her Con Law mid-term, but I wouldn't give her the time of day after she beat me out of the Am Jur Award in Tort Law.*

I wouldn't put it past him

Meaning: I would not doubt that he could accomplish that or would do that.

Example: *If you're wondering if Nate Underhill can make that 40-foot putt, I wouldn't put it past him; I really wouldn't.*

I wouldn't touch him/that with a ten-foot pole

Meaning: Because of the inherent risks, I will not go near or become involved with that person or activity.

Example: *That is a Social Media trap if I've ever seen one and without question, I wouldn't touch it with a ten-foot pole.*

I wouldn't want to be in (someone's) shoes

Meaning: That person is, or those persons are, in trouble and I do not envy their predicament.

Example: *The United States does not tolerate terrorists— particularly ones who overtly threaten American lives—and I wouldn't want to be in his shoes.*

Jack-of-all-trades

Meaning: Competent in several independent and distinct specialties.

Example: *As a doctor, engineer and poet, people regularly commented that Jeramiah Mitchell was a Jack-of-all-trades.*

Jockey for position

Meaning: Maneuver in relation to competitors to gain an advantage.

Example: *William Honeypen III was jockeying for position before the start of the hot dog-eating competition, arranging his water cups, adjusting the position of his paper plate, flexing his stomach and giving his competitors the thousand-yard stare.*

Jog (one's) memory

Meaning: Using something—a word, a general subject, a train of thought, for example, to refresh one's memory about something observed, experienced or spoken about.

Example: *Sorry, but I was distracted by that gunshot—can you jog my memory on what I was just saying?*

Johnny-on-the-spot

Meaning: Present at just the right moment to be helpful.

Example: *Priscilla was Johnny-on-the-spot to help extricate her friend, Tommy, from his awkward position upside down and sideways on the jungle-gym.*

John Q. Public

Meaning: The quintessential common person.

Example: *John Q. Public in Australia would probably not take kindly to the government rounding up unvaccinated people and "quarantining" them in what amount to prisons—particularly considering that the threat from the Covid virus has proved to have been roughly akin to that of an annual flu and the health hazard from the mRNA vaccines is real and exceptionally serious.*

Johnny-come-lately

Meaning: A person unfavorably delayed in arrival, yet expecting to be considered as on time.

Example: *Karen was a Johnny-come-lately to the School Board hearings concerning weapons on campus, but she insisted on arguing for second chances and rehabilitation, even as to firearms violations.*

Join the club

Meaning: We're all in similar circumstances.

Example: *You think you're the only one with money problems these days—well, join the club.*

Judge, jury and executioner

Meaning: A person who decides not only what the "facts" are, but then enforces their opinion of the facts against someone.

Example: *When Jerry's dad found our stash of fire crackers and cherry bombs, he became Judge, jury and executioner as he confiscated everything and made sure we never found it again.*

Jump on the bandwagon

Meaning: To join into a movement of some type, especially after it has already gained momentum.

Example: *Once the actors' union voted to go on strike, the writer's union jumped on the bandwagon, voting to support the actors and to not cross their picket lines.*

Jump ship

Meaning: Leave a weak or failing organization to improve one's situation.

Example: *The aging lawyers jumped ship at the inimitable Smith Law Firm and joined a younger firm on the rise.*

Jump the gun

Meaning: Start an activity prematurely.

Example: *Bill Ventura jumped the gun when he stood up after the bottom of the Sixth Inning and started singing, at the top of his lungs, Take Me Out to the Ball Game.*

Jump the track

    Meaning: To unexpectedly divert from progress in accomplishing a goal.

    Example: *Unfortunately, when City Treasurer, Mildred Whistlepoof, resumed her fiscal address to the City Council, she jumped the track and rambled on about dandelions and clover grass.*

Jump through hoops

    Meaning: To accomplish relatively mundane tasks in order to arrive at the principal objective.

    Example: *The worst part of buying real estate is having to jump through hoops in applying for the mortgage loan.*

Jump to conclusions

    Meaning: To prematurely extrapolate from insufficient preliminary data to significant assumptions of fact.

    Example: *We simply don't know enough information to determine the cause of the helicopter crash, so please do not jump to conclusions from the sketchy reports to date.*

The jury is out

    Meaning: The matter is still undecided.

    Example: *If you're wondering whether my character will recur in the drama,* Alien World, *the jury is still out but we should find out soon.*

Justice is blind

    Meaning: The overall system of justice is

non-discriminatory regarding suspect and quasi-suspect classifications such as race, gender, religion, national origin, alienage (for legal aliens) and sexual orientation.

Example: *Don't tell me "justice is blind" when you don't even know what life be like in da hood.*

Just in the nick of time

Meaning: Accomplished or occurring close to the last feasible moment before something can be changed or something negative will occur.

Example: *Racing across town and risking multiple traffic tickets including a carpool lane violation, I made it just in the nick of time to the filing window of the Court of Appeals.*

Just might could

Meaning: A Southern United States expression for, maybe I will sometime.

Example: *If you're askin' whether I'm available to attend your Ice Cream Social this Saturday afternoon, well then yes, I just might could.*

Just what the doctor ordered

Meaning: Exactly what was needed for the situation.

Example: *It was unseasonably hot that August day in Lancaster, California—the thermometer read 105 degrees in the shade—and two double-scooped ice cream cones were just what the doctor ordered for my daughter and me.*

Kangaroo Court

Meaning: A biased adjudication in which a predetermined result is given some aura of ostensible legitimacy through a *pro forma* proceeding in which the litigant or an interested party has few if any procedural rights and no chance of prevailing on the merits of the dispute.

Example: *The parole review hearing was in reality a Kangaroo Court in which the Board was bound and determined to find the inmate suitable for parole, despite any danger he presented to the community upon his release from prison.*

Keel over

Meaning: To pass out, become unconscious.

Example: *I was laughing so hard, I almost keeled over when he fell into the swimming pool in his Sunday suit.*

Keep a cool head

Meaning: Stay calm under pressure.

Example: *Okay guys, keep a cool head, play heads up ball and you can beat them, no problem.*

Keep an eye out for (someone or something)
   Meaning: Be watching for someone or something to appear.
   Example: *With the Child Abduction Alert all over the airwaves, the Highway Patrol vehicle was prominently parked on the freeway overpass for the officer to keep an eye out for a light blue, 1965 Chevy Nova.*

Keep a stiff upper lip
   Meaning: Be emotionally strong in the face of adversity and try not to appear upset.
   Example: *If he sees you being sad, then he wins twice, so keep a stiff upper lip and when this is over, we go for ice cream.*

Keep a straight face
   Meaning: Refrain from smiling regardless of what was being said or done at the time.
   Example: *Depending on the actor you're working with, it can be very difficult if not impossible to keep a straight face on every take of a funny scene.*

Keep a tab on/Keep tabs on
   Meaning: To follow the trail of someone or something.
   Example: *I wanted to keep a tab on Chanise Jones because there was something about her presence which was very marketable.*

Keep (someone) at arm's length
   Meaning: Refrain from allowing one's personal friendship

or other relationship, with the other party in a transaction, to affect the outcome.

Example: *Jeremy had to learn the hard way keep his estranged wife at arm's length in the divorce proceeding, and he ended up leaving a lot of money on the table.*

Keep it under your vest/hat

Meaning: Refrain from revealing particular things to anyone.

Example: *We got a big play coming up tomorrow, a real big play over at Tech-Tron but I want you to keep it under your vest.*

Keep (one's) nose clean

Meaning: Stay out of trouble.

Example: *Listen, Jimmy, if you keep your nose clean for another three months—just three lousy months—then you're off formal probation clean as a whistle and there's no more supervision.*

Keep (one's) nose to the grindstone

Meaning: Continue working diligently.

Example: *My daddy always said to keep my nose to the grindstone, but my mama told me, "Don't try an' do everything in a single day."*

Keep (someone) on their toes

Meaning: Do something to keep a person sharp and focused in a particular activity or undertaking.

Example: *To keep the young law student on her toes in Tuesday's Tort class, I asked her to succinctly describe the facts in the* Palsgraf v. Long Island Railroad Company *case.*

Keep (someone) posted
Meaning: Update a particular person, from time to time, on some circumstance, activity or event.
Example: *Kirsten, I have nothing for you in your job category today but I'll gladly keep you posted if you check back in a week or so.*

Keep the wolf from the door
Meaning: Guard against debt collectors or against going into heavy debt.
Example: *Tina was in tears when she finally admitted to her four, teen-aged children that she's having a real hard time keeping the wolf from the door.*

Keep (something) under wraps
Meaning: Make efforts to conceal something from detection by others.
Example: *Keep the breach under wraps for the time being—at least until we know whether the cargo was damaged.*

Keep your chin up
Meaning: Be emotionally strong in the face of adversity and try not to appear upset.
Example: *Keep your chin up Buddy, 'cause there are better*

dames in the world out there than that broad with the phony wig and the cheap perfume.

Keep your eye on the ball

Meaning: Stay focused on the effectiveness of one's work and success of the project.

Example: *We'd been on the stake-out for eleven hours straight when our backup finally arrived, and I gotta admit that after that long, it's tough to keep your eye on the ball.*

Keep your eyes peeled

Meaning: Be very observant for a particular thing.

Example: *Okay boys, this is it, so keep your eyes peeled for a mid-30s Cubano with a moustache and a slight limp.*

Keep your fingers crossed

Meaning: Be hopeful for good luck and a good result.

Example: *Here come the numbers, baby, so keep your fingers crossed and maybe this week we win it all!*

Keep your pants on

Meaning: Don't be so impatient.

Example: *I was fumbling with my change and the receipt, and the guy behind me was nudging me away from the counter, so I told him to keep his pants on.*

Keep your shirt on

Meaning: Be patient and calm down.

Example: *Hey, friendo, you wanna keep your shirt on there, or you gonna have some trouble with me?*

Kick ass and take names

Meaning: Work hard and take care of whatever needs to be done.

Example: *Oh man, oh man it was such a great feelin', kickin' ass and takin' names, just like the old days working for the Herald.*

Kick the bucket

Meaning: To die.

Example: *Moments before the old guy kicked the bucket, he whispered in my ear, "Find the treasure chest and it's yours, it's yours!"*

Kicked (someone) to the curb

Meaning: Fired from a job or terminated from some kind of relationship.

Example: *My girlfriend, Wendy, kicked me to the curb when she learned about Sara Sue.*

Kill the goose that lays the golden egg

Meaning: In trying to improve something, to cut yourself off from the actual source of income or prosperity.

Example: *Benny, Benny slow down, think a bit and stop criticizing the Boss at every turn, 'cause you don't wanna kill the goose that lays the golden egg.*

Kill two birds with one stone

> **Meaning:** Accomplish multiple tasks with a single effort of some kind.
>
> **Example:** *By filing for a Conservatorship of the Person and Estate of Xavier Sinterbaum, we kill two birds with one stone, since we create a defense for your prior suspect acts and we position you for taking lawful control of his financial affairs.*

King's ransom

> **Meaning:** An exorbitant amount of money.
>
> **Example:** *The contractor had us over a barrel with all of the design changes we'd implemented and it demanded what amounted to a king's ransom for the latest batch of Change Orders.*

Kiss (something) goodbye

> **Meaning:** It's gone now; it's no longer accessible.
>
> **Example:** *Once the producer figured out I was a Republican, I knew I could kiss that role goodbye—but then she surprised me, confiding that she was a closet-Republican herself.*

Kiss of death

> **Meaning:** Something said or done which marks the surefire end to or failure of an activity or project.
>
> **Example:** *Buying sweet Red Delicious apples as ingredients in an apple pie was the kiss of death, and his mother sent young Benjamin back to the market to replace them with tart, Granny Smith apples, which are much better in holding their shape during baking.*

Kitty corner

Meaning: Diagonal from where one is presently located.

Example: *In this blink-and-you'll-miss-it small town, the Mini-Mart was conveniently located kitty corner from the old-style, gasoline-only gas station.*

Knee-high to a grasshopper

Meaning: Very short, compared to an adult.

Example: *Why, Shirley-May was the cutest little thing—knee-high to a grasshopper, dressed in jeans and a tee-shirt and ready for fun.*

Knee-jerk reaction

Meaning: A spontaneous, and poorly thought-out, response to some observation or announcement.

Example: *The officer's knee-jerk reaction was that I was a hit-and-run driver, but when I showed her my car was damaged to the point of being immovable, she reevaluated the situation and calmed down.*

Knock on wood

Meaning: A superstitious expression (or the action of actually knocking on something wooden), intended to avoid the bad luck believed to follow from stating affirmatively or implying that some particular thing will or will not occur.

Example: *One more out, and Blade Decker will have pitched a perfect game, knock on wood.*

Knock your socks/block off

Meaning: Astound you.

Example: *This kid, by the time he was thirteen years of age, would knock your socks off with his fielding and hitting abilities.*

(To) know full well

Meaning: To clearly and obviously know or be aware of something.

Example: *The jerk knew full well that Shirley would suffer profound humiliation and sorrow if he exposed her accidental mistreatment of her horse, Barney, but nevertheless, the blabbermouth described it in great detail to several of her friends.*

(To) know (something) like the back of (one's) hand

Meaning: Exceptionally familiar with how something looks or operates.

Example: *Randal didn't want to boast, but the fact was that he knew the ins and outs of that computer virus like the back of his hand, and within a few keystrokes, the virus was dead as a doornail.*

Know (one's) place

Meaning: Understand where one stands in the particular hierarchy.

Example: *Gerda was an incredibly kind, effective and appreciated nanny for her wealthy, television-star clients, but she knew her place and tactfully avoided getting in-between the couple in marital disputes.*

Lambs to the slaughter

Meaning: Innocent and helpless victims heading for disaster.

Example: *Having yielded all of their firearms and ammunition to the federal government, the citizens of Adunda were lambs to the slaughter when the Climate Change Death-lottery law was enacted.*

The last/final nail in the coffin

Meaning: An action or omission which causes something to fail, which had already begun to fail.

Example: *The final nail in the coffin was when a victim recognized a ring—her husband's ring with his initials on the inside—on the hand of one of the burglary defendants during the preliminary hearing.*

The last minute

Meaning: Very close in time just before the final opportunity to do something.

Example: *Yesterday morning at 7 a.m., I got a last minute, panic call from a casting director who asked if I could be on the set of* Uptown is Downtown *in one hour as a replacement actor, and of course I said that I'd be there.*

The last straw

Meaning: The final negative event to precipitate a response.

Example: *When Mortimer Elderberry refused to take piccolo lessons, that was the last straw for his girlfriend, Matilda Tuber, and she unceremoniously kicked him to the curb.*

Laughing stock

Meaning: A person who is the object of popular ridicule.

Example: *This laughing stock woman became a poster-child of ridicule after she criticized a 55-year-old man for being attracted to a sensuous 25-year-old woman.*

(To) lawyer up

Meaning: In the face of accusations or threat of investigation or prosecution, to seek out and follow the advice of an attorney.

Example: *Alonzo was being peppered by two, ruthless detectives for answers, but the seasoned scofflaw abruptly decided to lawyer up, stating, "Okay, no more questions, 'cause I want my mouthpiece, my lawyer, here, and that's that."*

Lay of the land

Meaning: A broad overview and general understanding of an activity or undertaking.

Example: *The Marines sent out an elite three-man advance team to get the lay of the land in this region of the treacherous Hindu Kush mountains.*

Lay it all on the line

Meaning: To be completely open, detailed and truthful about a subject in order to prevail in some manner.

Example: *Listen, I'm gonna lay it all on the line for you, 'cause I wanna be totally transparent about my compulsive appetite for orange popsicles.*

Leading edge

Meaning: The most advanced of something such as technology, strategy or science.

Example: *The four brilliant graduate students were on the leading edge of astrophysics exploration.*

Leap of faith

Meaning: An action which, although not assured of success, represents a calculated risk with a reasonably favorable chance of positive results.

Example: *Inspired by the brilliance of guitarist Gabriella Quevedo and in a leap of faith, Jack embarked on a mastery of Chicago's, "Hard to Say I'm Sorry," despite it being several levels of difficulty above his current guitar acumen.*

Learn it by heart

Meaning: A throwback to ancient times when it was believed that one's thoughts and decisions were made in one's heart—to *memorize* something word-for-word.

Example: *An amateur will memorize something by reading it over and over to themselves, but a professional actor will learn it by heart through speaking the material in larger and larger pieces, understanding its meaning and context, and knowing it as if it were being said in real life, thereby turning the basis of it into an* actual memory.

(To) learn the hard way

Meaning: To acquire knowledge about something through personally experiencing adverse consequences arising from a former lack of knowledge.

Example: *For this knucklehead, it looks like he is going to have to learn the hard way that you do NOT borrow money from me and then not pay the juice.*

Learn the ropes

Meaning: To acquire an understanding of the details of successfully undertaking a particular environment, task or job.

Example: *Sure, of course, I'd like to learn the ropes as a software programmer, but seriously, isn't it possible to do this at a coffee shop with a vanilla latte?*

Leave money on the table

Meaning: To profit substantially less in a transaction than would have been the result with fully competent bargaining efforts.

Example: *Unfortunately for the husband in the transaction, his* *lawyer left tens of thousands of Dollars on the table, primarily because he failed to consider the Arizona vacation home as being Quasi-Community Property.*

Leave no stone unturned

Meaning: Undertake and execute an extremely thorough search or investigation.

Example: *The veteran gumshoe promised the silky dame that he'd leave no stone unturned in finding the sap who killed her husband at the Five & Dime.*

Left and right

Meaning: All around.

Example: *We all looked left and right for our dog's favorite toy but just couldn't find it.*

Left-handed/back-handed compliment

Meaning: An insult masquerading as praise.

Example: *When the mid-20s girl commented that I was good looking for a short, middle-aged, balding man, it was obviously intended as a left-handed compliment.*

Left high and dry

Meaning: To be abandoned by another or others without the means of extricating one's self from an adverse situation.

Example: *Sara's girlfriends left her high and dry at the bar in Cancun, with no way back to their hotel except for a long walk on the beach alone, at night.*

The/a leopard can't change its spots

Meaning: Some bad behaviors are so ingrained that the person simply cannot improve.

Example: *I told you, warned you, to never associate with that guy—he's dangerous and unpredictable and a leopard can't change its spots.*

The lesser of two evils

Meaning: Given a choice between two undesirable alternatives, then opting for the more desirable of the two.

Example: *Prosecutors needed a snitch to sew up a conviction, so they chose the lesser of two evils, Buddy Whipple, to testify against his murderous partner-in-crime, Augusta Q. Finkel.*

Let alone

Meaning: And particularly not.

Example: *The attractive college co-ed looked the truck driver over and rudely responded to him, saying, "The fact is, that I wouldn't be interested in even knowing your name, let alone having dinner with you."*

Let bygones be bygones

Meaning: Allow things that have occurred in the distant past to be forgiven and forgotten.

Example: *The rival, youth baseball coaches decided to let bygones be bygones despite a season filled with ill-tempered remarks on both sides of the aisle.*

(To) let (someone) have it

Meaning: To vociferously and precipitously dump one's grievances on another person.

Example: *When her drunken husband poured himself through the front door of their house at 3:25 a.m. looking like something the cat drug in, Mable finally let him have it, and he slept that night on the living room couch.*

Let (someone) off the hook

Meaning: Absolve someone of the consequences of their wrongful actions.

Example: *The Sheriff's Deputy was sorely tempted to arrest the boy, but at the last minute he decided to let him off the hook with only a stern warning.*

Let's get (something) off the ground

Meaning: We should do what needs to be done to get a project started and eventually operational.

Example: *Okay, people, all major cryptos have struggled over the past week, so let's get our product off the ground with a strong crypto brokerage and social image.*

Let sleeping dogs lie

Meaning: If something is not currently creating a problem, refrain from confronting it.

Example: *Armando had hoped the LAPD would let sleeping dogs lie, but those hopes were dashed when two officers arrested* *him as the Freeway Bandit in a decades-old series of armed bank robberies.*

Let's table this

Meaning: We should temporarily postpone consideration of a particular issue.

Example: *The Board meeting was proceeding nicely toward its takeover bid vote, until Willard A. Grimsley, Junior suggested, "Let's table this until next month," at which moment chaos ensued.*

Let the cat out of the bag

Meaning: To inadvertently reveal something that had previously been concealed or otherwise undisclosed.

Example: *Third Grader Eunice Baker let the cat out of the bag when she drew attention to a satchel full of dark chocolate candies hidden below Miss Gingersnap's desk.*

Let the chips fall where they may

Meaning: Allow a result to occur that is in accordance with all of the pertinent facts and circumstances.

Example: *Mister Humadinger had the authority to pay more than was being offered, but he elected to let the chips fall where they may in salary arbitration for the All-Star shortstop.*

Let/after the dust settle(s)(d)

Meaning: An enhanced view of a particular situation once time passes and more details naturally emerge.

Example: *The jury was biased in favor of the prosecution from the very outset of the trial, but in deliberations and after the dust* *settled, they realized the immutable truth that defendant Ramirez was absolutely innocent of all charges.*

Let your guard down

Meaning: Relax one's situational awareness and ordinary caution.

Example: *The middle-aged black couple asking for simple directions caused Mortimer to let his guard down, and without seeing it coming, their accomplice tasered him, rendering him helpless to the ensuing robbery.*

Letter of the law

Meaning: A strict and literal implementation of a contract, law or ordinance.

Example: *Having endured seven months of unrelenting trouble from this litigious tenant, the owner directed his lawyer to enforce the rental agreement to the letter of the law in pursuing a prompt eviction.*

(One's) level best

Meaning: The very best, within reason, one can do or accomplish in a task.

Example: *Unfortunately for Miss Finzelpacker, her level best in preparing a Buttermilk Pie with Pecan Crust just wasn't up to snuff for the Gann Valley Fair in Buffalo County of South Dakota.*

Liars figure and figures lie

Meaning: Statistics should not be trusted without critical scrutiny, since their underlying definitions and assumptions can be manipulated so readily.

Example: *Robert refused to be swayed by the Media's statistics since, as he had stated previously on many occasions, liars figure and figures lie.*

Lie down with dogs and wake up with fleas

Meaning: If you associate or identify with undesirable people, their negative character traits may well begin to change you for the worse.

Example: *Judge Hornswaggle took the young criminal defense attorney aside and cautioned him against getting too emotionally aligned with his clients, pontificating fruitlessly that if you lie down with dogs, you wake up with fleas.*

Lie like a rug

Meaning: Fabricate profusely and unapologetically.

Example: It *was an absolute certainty—Benny Ward was a despicable con man who lied like a rug and failed to display any conscience whatsoever.*

Lies through his teeth

Meaning: Blatant, full-on prevarication without the slightest sense of regret.

Example: *This disgusting, sociopathic punk constantly and compulsively lies through his teeth, and wouldn't know the truth if it hit him over the head.*

Life and limb

>**Meaning:** Death or great bodily injury.
>
>**Example:** *Winston considered risking life and limb by jumping into the raging river, but instead, he ran alongside it and plucked the stray dog to safety as it drifted close to the edge.*

Lift a finger

>**Meaning:** Help even in the very slightest way.
>
>**Example:** *Marley refused to lift a finger to help Esmerelda with her prom dress, after her traitor-friend had stolen Marley's boyfriend.*

A light at the end of the tunnel

>**Meaning:** A solution to a problem or completion of a task is out there and obtainable.
>
>**Example:** *Ordinarily, after getting lost in the National Forest, there would be a light at the end of the tunnel, but once the hikers proceeded deeply into bear country without a rifle, their fate was all but sealed.*

Light on (one's) feet

>**Meaning:** Nimble and adroit.
>
>**Example:** *The soccer-mom was light on her feet, and when the opponent's shot-on-goal flew toward the sidelines, she deftly blocked it from striking her youngest daughter.*

Like a bat out of hell

>**Meaning:** Exceedingly fast.

Example: *When the German tourist, Charles Zimmerhoffen, realized that a large Tiger Shark had just passed within a few feet of him, he was out of the water like a bat out of hell and into the safety of the boat.*

Like a chicken with its head cut off

Meaning: Being so exasperated and stressed that one behaves irrationally and inefficiently.

Example: *He scoured the parking lot like a chicken with its head cut off, until finally, almost a hundred yards from the Mall entrance, he scored an open spot.*

Like a duck to water

Meaning: So naturally, as if it were instinctive.

Example: *Cole Bingham was a ranch hand by trade, but was in excellent shape and took to pickle ball like a duck to water.*

Like a ton of bricks

Meaning: A severe, figurative and usually negative impact.

Example: *After having diligently served her client's interests, being served with the malpractice action hit Anastasia Merlot like a ton of bricks.*

Like nobody's business

Meaning: Accomplished with a very high degree of skill and technical sophistication.

Example: *The 12-year-old could longboard surf like nobody's business and was a hit with all of his 7th Grade classmates.*

Like pulling teeth

Meaning: A task which is very, very difficult.

Example: *Getting the police officer to answer simple questions about the basis for the prolonged detention was like pulling teeth.*

Like riding a bike/As easy as riding a bike

Meaning: An activity or skill which once learned is later easily refreshed and brought current.

Example: *Don't worry about it, 'cause once you learn how to rob a bank, it's like riding a bike—you won't forget.*

Like there's no tomorrow

Meaning: With a pronounced sense of urgency.

Example: *When I learned that alien technology had been present here for decades, I decided to live life like there's no tomorrow.*

Like white on rice

Meaning: Exceedingly close in proximity to something.

Example: *Once the retired attorney volunteered for the election committee, he was like white on rice for every campaign task coming his way.*

Lion's share

Meaning: Most, or almost all, of something.

Example: *Willard received the lion's share of credit for the company's growth and financial strength, but his son, Louis, was clearly the driving force.*

Lip service

Meaning: Token and insincere verbal assertions.

Example: *The President's lip service supporting the health and well-being of the public gradually lost its effectiveness with an increasingly informed citizenry.*

A little bird told me

Meaning: Someone, whose identity is intentionally being concealed, informed me of a particular piece of information.

Example: *After the prisoner was found to have committed suicide under mysterious circumstances, a little bird told me that the death was actually orchestrated by a three-letter governmental agency.*

A little of this and a lot of that

Meaning: An intentionally vague description of the components of some particular thing.

Example: *In describing the Middle School curriculum and resources for its "Sex Education" course, the Principal placated the PTA assembly by advising that it encompassed a little of this and a lot of that.*

Live and let live

Meaning: Maintain a healthy tolerance for different cultures and lifestyle choices.

Example: *Some of Melinda's friends didn't want to hang out with Jessica, who last year was a boy named Jeff, but Melinda's attitude was "live and let live."*

Live by the sword, die by the sword

Meaning: If one chooses to succeed using a particular method, skill or tool, then that person should also realize that he or she might also fall due to the use of that method, skill or tool.

Example: *As the drunken, off-duty police officer was roughly hauled out of his SUV and placed under arrest by two Highway Patrol officers, he learned first-hand the meaning of "live by the sword, die by the sword."*

Live to fight another day

Meaning: Save yourself from complete and unmitigated defeat or failure in order that at some time in the future you can again attempt to compete and achieve your objectives.

Example: *In a 23-to-2 blow-out baseball game, the savvy Jayhawks Manager, Skipper Redmond, opted for the team to live to fight another day by saving the Bullpen and sending their back-up shortstop to the mound for the final three innings of play.*

Living hand-to-mouth

Meaning: Surviving day-to-day, with little or no savings or resources for the future.

Example: *The young street urchins were living hand-to-mouth every day, but were making a killing for their "Uncle" in a notorious pick-pocket enterprise.*

Living on borrowed time

Meaning: Destined to die soon due to injury, disease, old age or some threatened outside cause.

Example: *My grandma has lived a wonderful and exciting life, but right now, at 105 years of age, she's living on borrowed time.*

A loaded question

Meaning: A question with an undisclosed implication, heavy in emotional impact and meaning.

Example: *Bob's question in front of several party guests, "So, Mildred, how's your dog Skippy doing these days?" was a loaded question since he knew full well that Mildred had negligently caused Skippy to break a leg a week prior.*

Loan shark

Meaning: A person who loans money at usurious rates of interest.

Example: *His girlfriend was into the loan shark for nearly twenty grand, and after she promised to stop gambling, permanently, he paid the guy off with cash.*

Lock and load

Meaning: A firearms term for, rendering a firearm all ready to fire with the pull of a trigger; but also, generally, being totally ready to commence action.

Example: *The skilled lawyer was locked and loaded as he approached the podium for his Closing Argument to the attentive jury.*

Lodge a complaint

Meaning: Formally communicate, usually in writing or electronically, a grievance.

Example: *Five-year-old Freddie Freeman announced to the school Principal that he wanted to lodge a complaint against six-year-old Priscilla Post for not picking him for her kickball team.*

The Lone Ranger

Meaning: A person by themselves, without assistance.

Example: *Listen, just don't think you're the Lone Ranger just because your high school girlfriend found another guy—it happens, plain and simple.*

Long arm of the law

Meaning: The broad reach of law enforcement.

Example: *He mistakenly believed that fleeing to Costa Rica would protect him from embezzlement and grand theft charges, but the long arm of the law reaches almost everywhere and soon, the infamous Benny "Fat Fingers" Donnelly was behind bars in Miami, Florida.*

Long face

Meaning: A stoic expression.

Example: *Jim had a long face as he walked his aging dog into the vet's office, and it took a few days before he was able to smile again, now that Cinnamon was gone.*

Long in the tooth

Meaning: Describing a person or animal who/which is elderly.

Example: *The horse was long in the tooth and chronically lame, but rather than put him down, she turned him out to pasture at a* *ranch in Temecula, California.*

(Never/don't) look a gift horse in the mouth

Meaning: Don't complain if something valuable is about to be given to you.

Example: *The ace reporter from the Morning Star newspaper was startled to receive the illuminating photographs, but they turned his investigation in an entirely new direction and he wasn't about to look a gift horse in the mouth.*

Look before you leap

Meaning: Before you engage in a potentially dangerous activity, do some background checking to see what you're up against.

Example: *She warned him to look before he leaped, but Barney ignored that advice and invited her to move in with him at his understated home in Bakersfield, California.*

Look like death warmed over

Meaning: With a very grave appearance; beaten down.

Example: *The mixed martial artist looked like death warmed over, but he had made it through the preliminaries, with only one victory between himself and the World Championship title.*

Look out for number one

Meaning: Be sure to take adequate measures to protect yourself from harm.

Example: *It's good to be kind and compassionate to others, but believe me, you always gotta look out for number one.*

Loose cannon

Meaning: An unpredictable and potentially problematic person.

Example: *Little Pauly was such a massive strongman and a notorious loose cannon that the Outfit decided to put his lights out, once and for all.*

Loose end

Meaning: An as yet unattended-to significant detail of a project or situation.

Example: *The dock worker who witnessed the theft was a real liability—you might say he was a loose end—and they had to make sure, one way or another, that he wouldn't talk.*

Lord willin' an' the creek don't rise

Meaning: The thing referred to will actually happen, maybe.

Example: *Joe Stamos is the number one Vet in this part of the County, and if he says the mare's gonna make it through this sickness, then she will—Lord willin' and the creek don't rise.*

Lose face

Meaning: Sustain damage to one's reputation.

Example: *The Blackfoot was okay using a sixth pack horse to move supplies up to the winter cabin, but what he won't tolerate is*

losing face with you making this situation an issue at
the Reservation.

Lose track

Meaning: Forget, temporarily.

Example: *There were so many details to remember in preparing*
for the barbeque, I'll admit that I lost track of a few things, but the
party turned out to be a total success, with everyone
enjoying themselves.

Lose (one's) head

Meaning: Lose control of yourself, particularly under
stressful conditions.

Example: *When the I.C.U. physician came through the door to*
tell me that my mother had just passed away from a heart attack,
I absolutely lost my head, picked him up and threw him through
the door, telling him to work on her again—and the good news is
that they did get her heart started and she lived a happy life for
another five years after that.

Lose (one's) shirt

Meaning: To sustain a major financial loss.

Example: *Jeremiah Jones lost his shirt on the water pump*
innovation, but he made a killing licensing his personal flotation
device, heat-retaining pod.

Lose (one's) touch

Meaning: Over time or through lack of practice, to

gradually lose one's fine, complicated or otherwise sophisticated skill.

Example: *I thought that I still had my croquet skills well intact, but today my sweet, six-year-old daughter, Jennifer, proved to me that apparently, I've lost my touch.*

Lost in the shuffle

Meaning: Due to circumstances that are often unclear, to become overlooked, delayed or defeated in one's aspirations.

Example: *The ambitious young professor was incredibly popular with her students and graduate students alike, but seems to have been lost in the shuffle in tenure review.*

Lost (one's) marbles

Meaning: A crude (or sometimes, a light-hearted), description of a person who has become mentally ill or seriously irrational in their thinking or actions.

Example: *Finnerty P. Hornswoggle methodically sized up the long, par-putt but as it rolled past the hole, down the slope and into the water hazard, he completely lost his marbles, launching the offending putter into the awaiting pond.*

Lost touch with (someone)

Meaning: Over time, to have failed to stay in communication with a particular person.

Example: *Due to circumstances beyond his control, Pete had lost touch with his daughter, Toni, but was pleased as punch to meet her again after more than a decade apart.*

Love is blind

Meaning: Deep affection for someone can make you unable to see their negative character traits.

Example: *The fact that love is blind, keeps Family Law lawyers in perpetual business representing parties in divorce and child custody proceedings.*

Low-hanging fruit

Meaning: The easily accessible objects or goals which one seeks.

Example: *Overcoming candidates in your own party amounts to the low hanging fruit, and the real battle is beating the other party's incumbent candidate.*

Luck of the draw

Meaning: Random chance.

Example: *I'm not saying that getting booked in particular roles is mostly the luck of the draw, which it isn't, but I am saying that there's a helluva lotta luck that goes into financial success over the course of an acting career.*

AUTHOR BIO

JACK FORBES is a Los Angeles-based attorney, actor and writer, who has previously published *JACK'S HANDY LIST OF WORDS—607 Words That You Can't (or Shouldn't) Live Without*; *ACTING OUTSIDE THE LINES—Perilous Journeys in Pivotal Acting Scenes*; *DECONSTRUCTING THE CODE*; *JACK'S HANDY GUIDE TO TRUSTS—Staying Out of Court*; *QUESTIONING THE WORD—An Atheist Confronts Faith in God*; *Stand Your Ground, TO KILL OR NOT TO KILL, The Legal Limits of Safety* and *NATURAL LAW AND INALIENABLE HUMAN RIGHTS, A Pathway to Freedom and Liberty*. Jack grew up in Long Beach, California. His official website is www.actorjack-forbes.com and his acting credits and bio may also be viewed on www.imdb.com.